Postcolonial Witnessing

Also by Stef Craps

TRAUMA AND ETHICS IN THE NOVELS OF GRAHAM SWIFT: No Short-Cuts to Salvation

Postcolonial Witnessing

Trauma Out of Bounds

Stef Craps

Ghent University, Belgium

First published 2012
First published in paperback in 2015 by
PALGRAVE MACMILLAN

Palgrave Macmillan in the UK is an imprint of Macmillan Publishers Limited, registered in England, company number 785998, of Houndmills, Basingstoke, Hampshire RG21 6XS.

Palgrave Macmillan in the US is a division of St Martin's Press LLC, 175 Fifth Avenue, New York, NY 10010.

Palgrave Macmillan is the global academic imprint of the above companies and has companies and representatives throughout the world.

Palgrave® and Macmillan® are registered trademarks in the United States, the United Kingdom, Europe and other countries.

ISBN 978–0–230–23007–1   hardback
ISBN 978–1–137–54319–6   paperback

A catalogue record for this book is available from the British Library.
A catalog record for this book is available from the Library of Congress.

Typeset by MPS Limited, Chennai, India.

For Karen

Contents

Acknowledgements

In the course of researching and writing this book I have incurred personal and professional debts to numerous individuals and institutions.

Throughout this process I have had the good fortune of being surrounded by a wonderful group of colleagues in the English Department and the Department of Literary Studies at Ghent University, which has been as stimulating, nurturing, and dynamic a working environment as I could hope for. I am particularly grateful to Gert Buelens, Philippe Codde, Marysa Demoor, Sigi Jöttkandt, Pieter Vermeulen, and Kries Versluys. It was Kries's questioning of my postcolonial credentials during the interview that led to my initial appointment at Ghent that first gave me the idea of trying to reconcile my interest in trauma studies, which had preoccupied me during my PhD years, with the passion for postcolonial literature that I had mainly cultivated before then. If the rest is history, this is in no small part thanks to Gert, who has been a mentor, a friend, an ally, and an inspiration, both as a scholar and as a human being.

One of the joys of working on this book has been getting to meet and collaborate with many remarkable scholars pursuing related projects. I want to thank Ortwin de Graef, Sam Durrant, Robert Eaglestone, Roger Luckhurst, and Michael Rothberg—aka my personal dream team—for their enthusiastic participation in a collaborative research project on the future of trauma studies hosted by the Flemish Academic Centre for Science and the Arts in the spring of 2009. I am also profoundly grateful to Stathis Gourgouris, Marianne Hirsch, Andreas Huyssen, Gayatri Spivak, Diana Taylor, and Sonali Thakkar for the hospitality and generosity they showed me during my stay as a visiting scholar at Columbia University in 2009–2010, of which I have the fondest memories.

Other inspiring academic companions I met along the way include Salhia Ben-Messahel, Hans Bertens, Matt Boswell, Maurizio Calbi, Sarah Casteel, Marguérite Corporaal, Rick Crownshaw, Mikhal

Dekel, Odin Dekkers, Sarah De Mul, Shane Graham, Dave Gunning, Kathleen Gyssels, Rosanne Kennedy, Lewis Kirshner, Joost Krijnen, Dominick LaCapra, Alison Landsberg, Bénédicte Ledent, Vivian Liska, John McLeod, Stephen Morton, Dirk Moses, Amy Novak, Susana Onega, Diederik Oostdijk, Felicity Palmer, Esther Peeren, Jody Allen Randolph, Pallavi Rastogi, Ann Rigney, Antony Rowland, Ellen Rutten, Debarati Sanyal, Ronnie Scharfman, Jonathan Sell, Sarah Senk, Efraim Sicher, Max Silverman, Dawn Skorczewski, Lyndsey Stonebridge, Daria Tunca, Chris van der Merwe, Abigail Ward, Anne Whitehead, Louise Yelin, and Yasemin Yildiz. I thank them all for their interest in my work and for various forms of assistance and encouragement.

Thanks are also due to Paula Kennedy and Ben Doyle at Palgrave Macmillan, for their editorial guidance, patience, and efficiency.

Several institutions and organizations were instrumental in supporting me as I worked on the manuscript. I am grateful to Ghent University, the Research Foundation Flanders, the Flemish Academic Centre for Science and the Arts, the Institute for Comparative Literature and Society at Columbia University, the Fulbright Program, the Dan David Foundation at Tel Aviv University, and the Belgian American Educational Foundation.

I would also like to thank my parents and parents-in-law, my siblings and siblings-in-law, and my friends Sabine Lefever, Irmgard Vinck, Ortwin Joniaux, and Jan Troost, for bearing with me and for providing many happy distractions. My greatest debt, though, is to Karen Van Holm, light of my life, whose love and support mean the world to me. I dedicate this book to her.

Ghent, March 2012

Parts of Chapters 1, 2, and 4 were published as "Wor(l)ds of Grief: Traumatic Memory and Literary Witnessing in Cross-Cultural Perspective" in *Textual Practice* 24.1 (2010): 51–68. Chapter 5 appeared as "Learning to Live with Ghosts: Postcolonial Haunting and Mid-Mourning in David Dabydeen's 'Turner' and Fred D'Aguiar's *Feeding the Ghosts*" in *Callaloo* 33.2 (2010): 467–75. Different versions of Chapter 7 were published as "Linking Legacies of Loss: Traumatic Histories and Cross-Cultural Empathy in Caryl Phillips's *Higher Ground* and *The Nature of Blood*" in *Studies in the Novel* 40.1–2 (2008): 191–202 and "Jewish/Postcolonial Diasporas in the Work of Caryl Phillips" in

Metaphor and Diaspora in Contemporary Writing, ed. Jonathan P. A. Sell (Palgrave Macmillan, 2012), 135–50. Permission to use a picture of Freddy Tsimba's sculpture *Silhouette effacée 2*—made out of spent bullet casings collected over more than ten years of war in his native Congo—as a cover image was generously granted by the artist. The photo in question was taken and kindly provided by Philippe Louzon.

Introduction

Trauma theory is an area of cultural investigation that emerged in the early 1990s as a product of the so-called ethical turn affecting the humanities. It promised to infuse the study of literary and cultural texts with new relevance. Amid accusations that literary scholarship, particularly in its deconstructive, poststructuralist, or textualist guise, had become indifferent or oblivious to "what goes on in the real world" (the world outside the text: history, politics, ethics), trauma theory confidently announced itself as an essential apparatus for understanding "the real world" and even as a potential means for changing it for the better.

This epistemological and ethical programme is clearly laid out in the highly influential work of Cathy Caruth, one of the founding figures of trauma theory (along with Shoshana Felman, Dori Laub, Geoffrey Hartman, and Dominick LaCapra). In *Unclaimed Experience: Trauma, Narrative, and History* (1996), she argues that a textualist approach—one which insists that all reference is indirect—need not lead us away from history and into "political and ethical paralysis" (10). Quite the contrary, she claims, it can afford us unique access to history: "Through the notion of trauma . . . we can understand that a rethinking of reference is aimed not at eliminating history but at resituating it in our understanding, that is, at precisely permitting *history* to arise where *immediate understanding* may not" (11). Caruth conceives history as being inherently traumatic, and trauma as an overwhelming experience that resists integration and expression. According to her, conjoining a psychoanalytic view of trauma with a deconstructive vigilance regarding the indeterminacies of

1

representation in the analysis of texts that bear witness to traumatic histories can grant us a paradoxical mode of access to extreme events and experiences that defy understanding and representation. In this account, textual "undecidability" or "unreadability" comes to reflect the inaccessibility of trauma.

Moreover, this critical practice comes invested with ethical significance. Caruth claims that the "new mode of reading and of listening" (9) that trauma demands can help break the isolation imposed on both individuals and cultures by traumatic experience: "history, like trauma, is never simply one's own, ... history is precisely the way we are implicated in each other's traumas" (24). In a catastrophic age such as ours, she writes elsewhere, "trauma itself may provide the very link between cultures" ("Trauma and Experience" 11). With trauma forming a bridge between disparate historical experiences, so the argument goes, listening to the trauma of another can contribute to cross-cultural solidarity and to the creation of new forms of community.

Remarkably, however, the founding texts of the field (including Caruth's own work) largely fail to live up to this promise of cross-cultural ethical engagement. They fail on at least four counts: they marginalize or ignore traumatic experiences of non-Western or minority cultures, they tend to take for granted the universal validity of definitions of trauma and recovery that have developed out of the history of Western modernity, they often favour or even prescribe a modernist aesthetic of fragmentation and aporia as uniquely suited to the task of bearing witness to trauma, and they generally disregard the connections between metropolitan and non-Western or minority traumas. As a result of all of this, rather than promoting cross-cultural solidarity, trauma theory risks assisting in the perpetuation of the very beliefs, practices, and structures that maintain existing injustices and inequalities.

The urgency of overcoming trauma theory's Eurocentric biases has recently been underlined by Jane Kilby, who states that while the future of trauma theory is to a large extent unpredictable, "for certain the question of globalization will dominate" (181). In arguing the need for trauma theory to be globalized more thoroughly and responsibly, this book aims to help make this prognosis a reality. In what follows, I will try to back up the criticisms just levelled, propose possible solutions, and illustrate my arguments using a range of literary examples. I will address each of the four aforementioned points in turn: first the marginalization of non-Western and minority traumas, then the supposed universal validity of Western definitions of trauma, next the problem of normative trauma aesthetics, and finally the underexplored relationship between First and Third World traumas.

Chapter 1 notes that trauma theory as a field of cultural scholarship developed out of an engagement with Holocaust testimony, literature, and history. It surveys the founding texts of the field—works published in the 1990s by scholars such as Caruth, Felman and Laub, Hartman, and LaCapra—to find that they tend to show little interest in traumatic experiences of members of non-Western cultural traditions; that is, people living outside hegemonic, wealthy nations or regions such as the United States, (Western) Europe, Canada, and Australia, as well as postcolonial indigenous groups and disempowered racial and diasporic groups living in Western countries. Trauma theory's failure to give the sufferings of those belonging to non-Western or minority groups due recognition sits uneasily with the field's ethical aspirations. While calling on trauma theory to broaden its usual focus, the chapter also cautions that the traumas of non-Western or minority populations need to be acknowledged for their own sake. As I show with reference to a number of scenes of cross-cultural witnessing in Caruth's *Unclaimed Experience*, rather than reflecting a postcolonial sensibility, well-meaning attempts to reach out to the racial, ethnic, or cultural other can effectively result in the appropriation or instrumentalization of his or her suffering in the service of articulating the trauma of the self.

In Chapter 2, I contend that the traumas of non-Western or minority groups must also be acknowledged on their own terms—another area where trauma theory has tended to fall short. Though widely considered a single, uniform, timeless, and universal phenomenon, the concept of psychological trauma is a Western artefact determined by its origins in a variety of late-nineteenth- and early-twentieth-century medical and psychological discourses dealing with Euro-American experiences of industrialization, gender relations, and modern warfare. Hegemonic definitions of trauma have been criticized for being culturally insensitive and exclusionary, and charges of cultural imperialism have been levelled at the uncritical cross-cultural application of Western trauma concepts in the context of international humanitarian disaster relief programmes. Arguing that dominant conceptions of trauma and recovery need to be revised and expanded if they are to adequately address the hitherto disregarded or overlooked psychological pain suffered by many disenfranchised groups, I turn to the pioneering work on the psychological effects of racism and colonialism by Frantz Fanon and to recent research by mental health professionals on the specificities of trauma in non-Western settings in search of alternative conceptualizations of trauma attuned to (post)colonial conditions. Drawing on such notions as "insidious trauma," "oppression-based trauma," "postcolonial syndrome," and "post-traumatic slavery syndrome," I elaborate a supplementary model of trauma which—unlike the traditional individual and event-based model—can account for and respond to collective, ongoing, everyday forms of traumatizing violence.

These concerns, and the alternative paradigms that have been proposed, have so far received very little attention from within the field of cultural trauma research, which for the most part continues to adhere to the traditional event-based model of trauma, according to which trauma results from a single, extraordinary, catastrophic event. For example, while LaCapra's work seeks to bring conceptual clarity to the field of trauma theory, his key distinction between loss (a psycho-historical experience related to a singular event) and absence (a structural, non-historical condition) is found to obscure the kind of long-term, cumulative trauma suffered by victims of racism or other forms of structural oppression, which fits neither category. This is not to say, though, that I agree with the idea that the field is irredeemably tainted with Eurocentric bias. Even though the main methodologies from which trauma theory takes its inspiration—psychoanalysis and deconstruction—have been accused of being fatally compromised by their (supposed) European provenance, I maintain that trauma theory can and should be reshaped, resituated, and redirected so as to foster attunement to previously unheard suffering.

Chapter 3 challenges the hegemonic pretensions of the dominant "trauma aesthetic": the notion, which has become all but axiomatic within trauma theory, that traumatic experiences can only be adequately represented through the use of experimental, modernist textual strategies. Trauma theorists tend to justify their preference for fragmented, non-linear, anti-narrative forms by pointing to similarities with the psychic experience of trauma. However, attempts to construct a normative trauma aesthetic create a narrow canon of valued trauma literature, consisting of high-brow, avant-garde works by mostly Western writers (for example, Paul Celan, W. G. Sebald, Charlotte Delbo, and Jonathan Safran Foer). I neither reject modernist modes of representation as inherently Eurocentric nor uphold any particular alternative as a postcolonial panacea, but I do stress the need to check the rush to dismiss whatever deviates from the prescribed aesthetic as regressive or irrelevant. Rather than positing a necessary relation between aesthetic form and political or ethical effectiveness, I argue that trauma theory should take account of the specific social and historical contexts in which trauma narratives are produced and received, and be open and attentive to the diverse strategies of representation and resistance that these contexts invite or necessitate.

The two chapters that follow illustrate the contribution that a "decolonized" trauma theory can make to our understanding of postcolonial literature that bears witness to the suffering engendered by racial or colonial oppression. Chapter 4 analyses South African writer Sindiwe Magona's novel *Mother to Mother* (1999 [1998]), a fictionalized account of the 1993 murder of white American Fulbright scholar Amy Biehl by a group of poor, young black men, which can be seen to negotiate the different conceptions of trauma outlined in Chapter 2. Narrated by the mother of the killer, the novel shows that a proper understanding of this spectacular event requires a full appreciation of the traumatizing impact of the "ordinary," structural violence inflicted on black South Africans by apartheid. I read Magona's novel as an implicit critique of the tendency of the Truth and Reconciliation Commission—which it shares with trauma theory in its classical formulation—to map Euro-American concepts of trauma and recovery straightforwardly onto an apartheid-colonial situation.

In Chapter 5, I examine the inscription of racial trauma in two literary works by contemporary British Caribbean writers that memorialize the Middle Passage, a history that has come to epitomize the experience of people of African descent throughout the Atlantic world: David Dabydeen's epic poem "Turner" (2002 [1995]) and Fred D'Aguiar's novel *Feeding the Ghosts* (1998 [1997]). These texts conjure the ghosts of victims of racial violence without, ultimately, conjuring them away in the name of a supposedly redeemed present, free from the burdens of the past. Both resist the temptation to leave the reader with the sense that the story has been told, consigned to the past; that it has been taken care of and can therefore now be forgotten. Rather than affirming a clear distinction between the past and the present, they demonstrate how those two are imbricated in one another: the past continues to structure the present; racist attitudes and practices persist throughout the ages. Thus, Dabydeen and D'Aguiar challenge traditional, Eurocentric concepts of trauma, mourning, and recovery that risk obscuring the continuing oppressive effects of the traumas of colonialism.

If trauma theory is to live up to its promise of cross-cultural ethical engagement, traumatic colonial histories not only have to be acknowledged more fully, on their own terms, and in their own terms, but they also have to be considered in relation to traumatic metropolitan or First World histories. Chapter 6 investigates the inherent relationality of history and trauma by looking at how various theorists have construed the relationship between the Holocaust—an atrocity committed in Europe, by Europeans, against Europeans—and other modern cataclysms. I examine attempts to theorize the co-implication of Holocaust and colonial trauma against the background of, firstly, the recent broadening of the focus of the field of memory studies—of which trauma theory is a subfield—from the national to the transnational level, and, secondly, efforts to bridge a disciplinary divide between Jewish and postcolonial studies preventing the Holocaust and histories of slavery and colonial domination from being considered in a common frame. Special attention is given to reviewing and critically assessing the arguments about the globalization of Holocaust memory advanced by Daniel Levy and Natan Sznaider, and by Jeffrey Alexander, and to describing the new model of remembrance developed in the recent work of Michael Rothberg, which recognizes that memories of different traumatic histories overlap, intertwine, and mutually influence each other.

The final two chapters examine how literature reflects and elicits a relational understanding of trauma by analysing a number of literary texts in which the legacies of the Holocaust and colonialism come into contact. In Chapter 7, I explore the links between histories of black and Jewish suffering in the work of the British Caribbean writer Caryl Phillips. In his novels *Higher Ground* (1989) and *The Nature of Blood* (1997), as well as in his travel book *The European Tribe* (1987), Phillips interweaves stories of anti-Semitic and racist violence set in many different times and places. I argue that his work seeks to foster attunement to multiple histories of suffering by supplementing a metaphorical view of history, which, in its insistence on similarity, threatens to conflate distinct historical experiences, with a metonymical view, which places them alongside one another and thus preserves the distance between them. Phillips's work presents a fuller picture of the dark underside of modernity, and it offers a compelling reflection on how mnemonic connections are to be made for visions of cross-cultural solidarity and justice rather than discord and violence to arise from them.

In Chapter 8, I discuss the resonances between the Holocaust, colonialism, and the Partition of the Indian subcontinent in Indian writer Anita Desai's novel *Baumgartner's Bombay* (1998 [1988]). The story centres on the life of a German Jew who emigrates to India in flight from the Nazis; is imprisoned as an enemy alien in a British internment camp for the length of the war; is delivered into the chaos and escalating violence of pre-Partition Calcutta upon his release; and lives out the rest of his life, poor and lonely, in a Bombay slum, where in his old age he is murdered by a young German drug addict. Through the figure of the Jewish refugee, *Baumgartner's Bombay* identifies and critiques forms and practices of what Paul Gilroy calls "camp-thinking" (*Between Camps*) wherever and whenever they manifest themselves in the modern era. I read Desai's novel as a study in cross-cultural incomprehension which reveals how the tendency to understand the sufferings of different victim groups only in particularistic terms can lead to or perpetuate conflict and hatred, and which calls upon the reader to transcend the divisions of camp-thinking.

I end this book by offering some concluding reflections on the importance and relevance of rethinking trauma theory from a postcolonial perspective in the globalized world of the twenty-first century. I discuss a number of incisive critiques of our contemporary "trauma culture" and its tendency towards spectacularization and sentimentalization of suffering, and I counter these with more positive appraisals of the political value of loss, trauma, and mourning, and of cultural inquiry into those issues. I suggest that, rather than serving as the handmaiden of the status quo or a purveyor of voyeuristic thrills, a decolonized trauma theory can act as a catalyst for meaningful change. By enabling us to recognize and attend to the sufferings of people around the world, an inclusive and culturally sensitive trauma theory can expose situations of injustice and abuse, and open up ways to imagine a different global future.

1
The Trauma of Empire

Broadening the focus

As Rebecca Saunders points out, "while trauma theory has primarily been produced in Europe and the United States, trauma itself has, with equal if not greater regularity and urgency, been experienced elsewhere" (15). However, most attention within trauma theory has been devoted to events that took place in Europe or the United States, especially the Holocaust and, more recently, 9/11. In fact, the impetus for much of the current theorization about trauma and representation was provided by the Nazi genocide of the European Jews (Kacandes 99; Kaplan, *Trauma Culture* 1; Bennett and Kennedy 3; Douglas and Whitlock 1). Indeed, trauma theory as a field of cultural scholarship developed out of an engagement with Holocaust testimony, literature, and history.

The work of Cathy Caruth, which has been singularly influential in setting the parameters of this new area of scholarship, is a case in point. Her central insight about the incompletion in knowing that is at the heart of trauma is indebted to Dori Laub's seminal thesis about "the collapse of witnessing," developed in relation to the Holocaust (Arruti 2). While Caruth acknowledges that Laub's remarks about the inability to fully witness the event as it occurs define "a specific quality of the Holocaust in particular which we would not wish too quickly to generalize," she goes on to do exactly that, noting how this Holocaust-specific quality "seems oddly to inhabit all traumatic experience" ("Trauma and Experience" 7).

Together with Shoshana Felman, Laub—a psychiatrist who has worked with Holocaust survivors, is himself one, and co-founded the Fortunoff Video Archive for Holocaust Testimonies at Yale University—published the landmark study *Testimony: Crises of Witnessing in Literature, Psychoanalysis, and History* (1992), which contains the text by Laub to which Caruth refers. Like one of the chapters contributed by Felman, this piece originally appeared in 1991 in a special issue of the journal *American Imago*, edited by Caruth and later included in her important collection *Trauma: Explorations in Memory* (1995). Though Felman occasionally uses the phrase "history as holocaust" (95; 105), suggesting a broad historical outlook, in actual fact *Testimony* deals almost exclusively with the Holocaust. Tellingly, the final chapter has a section titled "Heart of Darkness" (240–42), but whereas Joseph Conrad's novella describes colonial atrocities in the Congo Free State (what Adam Hochschild and others have called "the African Holocaust"), Felman invokes Conrad's title to refer to Nazi evils—specifically, the darkened interior of Nazi gas vans.

That Dominick LaCapra's interest in issues of trauma arose out of his engagement with the historiography of the Holocaust is clear from the titles of the first two books in which he turns his attention to trauma: *Representing the Holocaust: History, Theory, Trauma* (1994) and *History and Memory after Auschwitz* (1998). The Holocaust remains the central point of reference in *Writing History, Writing Trauma* (2001), which, however, explores the role of trauma in history-writing more generally.[1] As LaCapra says in the preface, "The Nazi genocide remains a crucial concern, but often problems are formulated more broadly as they bear on the role of trauma in and across history" (x). Slavery, apartheid, and the atomic bombing of Hiroshima and Nagasaki are occasionally mentioned alongside the Holocaust—for example, as additional instances of "founding trauma" (81)—but in general these other histories play a very limited role in the book. Asked, in an interview for Yad Vashem that serves as the final chapter, whether the "overemphasis" on the Holocaust in the United States is "some kind of denial" of traumas closer to home, such as slavery and the genocide of the Native Americans, LaCapra says that this may well be the case (171). He goes on to note some important differences between slavery and the Holocaust, but concludes that "[s]lavery, like the Holocaust, nonetheless presents, for a people, problems of traumatization, severe oppression, a divided heritage, the question of a founding trauma, the forging of identities in the present, and so forth" (174).

  Geoffrey Hartman's main contribution to trauma theory is his work on Holocaust video testimony, produced in the context of his involvement with the Fortunoff Video Archive, which he co-founded (see, e.g. "The Humanities of Testimony"; "Memory.com"; and "Shoah and Intellectual Witness"). The "optics" of testimony that Hartman develops in these writings is informed by his career-long investment in the poetry of William Wordsworth: video testimony, for Hartman, functions as an update of Wordsworth's poetical practice for a visual age (Vermeulen). In *The Fateful Question of Culture* (1997), he makes the rather breathtaking claim that Wordsworth's poetic intervention in the traumatic transition from a traditional, rural society to a modern, urban one may be credited with guarding England from national socialism and thus preventing an English Holocaust. He speculates that Wordsworth's mediation "saved English politics from the virulence of a nostalgic political ideal centering on rural virtue, which led to serious ravages on the continent" (7).[2] While Hartman claims "no more than heuristic value" for his startling thesis, in the next sentence he turns it into an article of faith, invulnerable to empirical attack and beyond the need of proof: "But were my conjectures to be disproved or shown incapable of being proved, I would continue to feel as Mrs. Henshaw does, in Willa Cather's *My Mortal Enemy*: 'How the great poets shine on...! Into all the dark corners of the world. They have no night'" (7). As Pieter Vermeulen has shown, in his work on Holocaust video testimony, Hartman tends to theorize that genre as "a contemporary instantiation of Wordsworth's saving mediation," with the same potential to ward off further genocidal violence (552–53). It is important to note, however, that Hartman's starting premise about England's successful avoidance of Holocaust-like trauma ignores the fact that, even if England has arguably to a large extent been spared the extreme violence that the European continent did inflict on itself, this has not prevented it from "export[ing] violence and suffering in the name of imperialism and colonialism or, more recently, a war on terror" (Vermeulen 564). Hartman's idealization of England as a trauma-free zone, which fails to take account of the trauma-ridden history of British imperialism that happened—and continues to happen—overseas, is symptomatic, it seems to me, of trauma theory's general blindness to, or lack of interest in, the traumas visited upon members of non-Western cultures.

This Eurocentric bias is rarely acknowledged by those subject to it. However, a notable exception is Jenny Edkins, who, in *Trauma and the Memory of Politics* (2003), admits that her study's

> focus is firmly on western conceptions of personhood and political community in the modern period. It does not examine, except in passing, how practices of trauma or memory may have been exported beyond what might be considered the geographical bounds of a western paradigm, nor does it discuss, except to point out the specificity of a western approach, how people seemingly located outside that paradigm differ in their practices. (9–10)

This lack of interest in the non-Western world is not unique, of course, to cultural critics but is shared by society at large. As Didier Fassin and Richard Rechtman point out in an anthropological study of trauma titled *The Empire of Trauma: An Inquiry into the Condition of Victimhood* (2009 [2007]), "trauma—or rather the social process of the recognition of persons as traumatized—effectively chooses its victims. Although those who promote the concept assert that it is universal, since it is the mark left by an event, study reveals tragic disparities in its use" (282). For example, humanitarian psychiatry—which I will have more to say about in the next chapter—for a long time ignored the African continent. While mental health support was already being routinely provided by Western aid workers to Croatians, Bosnians, Kosovars, Armenians, Romanians, Chechnyans, and Palestinians in the wake of natural disasters or political violence, Rwandans, Sierra Leoneans, Liberians, and Congolese—people long relegated to the margins of the circle of humanity—were initially denied such assistance in their hour of need (183–88; 282). Fassin and Rechtman also note that the 2004 tsunami in Thailand resulted in much greater international mobilization, including action around trauma, than the earthquake in Pakistan the following year, mainly because the tsunami affected Western tourists whereas no Westerners were involved in the earthquake (282). They explain these disparities as follows:

Recognition of trauma, and hence the differentiation between victims, is largely determined by two elements: the extent to which politicians, aid workers, and mental health specialists are able to identify with the victims, in counterpoint to the distance engendered by the otherness of the victims. Cultural, social, and perhaps even ontological proximity matter; as does the a priori valuation of the validity of the cause, misfortune, or suffering, a valuation that obviously implies a political and often an ethical judgment. Thus trauma, often unbeknownst to those who promote it, reinvents "good" and "bad" victims, or at least a ranking of legitimacy among victims. (282)

In a thoughtful article on the contexts, politics, and ethics of trauma theory, Susannah Radstone similarly observes that

it is the sufferings of those, categorized in the West as "other", that tend *not* to be addressed via trauma theory—which becomes in this regard, a theory that supports politicized constructions of those with whom identifications via traumatic sufferings can be forged and those from whom such identifications are withheld. (25)

Judith Butler spells out the far-reaching consequences of such constructions in *Frames of War: When Is Life Grievable?* (2009), where she argues that the differential distribution of precarity across populations is "at once a material and a perceptual issue": "those whose lives are not 'regarded' as potentially grievable, and hence valuable, are made to bear the burden of starvation, underemployment, legal disenfranchisement, and differential exposure to violence and death" (25). A one-sided focus on traumas suffered by members of Western cultural traditions could thus have pernicious effects at odds with trauma theory's self-proclaimed ethical mission. If trauma theory is to adhere to its ethical aspirations, the sufferings of those belonging to non-Western or minority cultures must be given due recognition. As Jill Bennett and Rosanne Kennedy write in the introduction to their edited collection *World Memory: Personal Trajectories in Global Time* (2003), trauma studies in the humanities "must move beyond its focus on Euro-American events and experiences, towards a study of memory that takes as its starting point the multicultural and diasporic nature of contemporary culture" (5).

The perils of appropriation

This is not to say, though, that any and all attempts by trauma theory to reach out to the non-Western other are necessarily a step in the right direction. After all, such efforts can turn out to reflect a Eurocentric bias just as well. This is true, for example, of the few descriptions of cross-cultural encounters that we are offered in Caruth's pioneering study *Unclaimed Experience*. I am thinking of her reading of the story of Tancred and Clorinda, her analysis of Sigmund Freud's *Moses and Monotheism*, and her interpretation of the film *Hiroshima mon amour*, all of which are central to her formulation of trauma theory, yet which strike me as highly problematic instances of witnessing across cultural boundaries.

Caruth's treatment of the story of Tancred and Clorinda has been analysed very incisively by Ruth Leys (292–97), Amy Novak (31–32), and Michael Rothberg (*Multidirectional Memory* 87–96), to whose work the brief discussion of it that I will offer is indebted. In the introduction to *Unclaimed Experience*, Caruth quotes the passage from *Beyond the Pleasure Principle* in which Freud discusses an episode from *Gerusalemme Liberata* (*Jerusalem Delivered*), a sixteenth-century epic by the Italian poet Torquato Tasso:

> Its hero, Tancred, unwittingly kills his beloved Clorinda in a duel while she is disguised in the armour of an enemy knight. After her burial he makes his way into a strange magic forest which strikes the Crusaders' army with terror. He slashes with his sword at a tall tree; but blood streams from the cut and the voice of Clorinda, whose soul is imprisoned in the tree, is heard complaining that he has wounded his beloved once again.
>
> (qtd. in Caruth, *Unclaimed Experience* 2)

Freud refers to this moment in the story as an example of the unconscious repetition of trauma: Tancred's unknowing killing of his beloved not just once, but twice, illustrates the repetition compulsion characteristic of trauma. Caruth expands upon Freud's reading of this moment, drawing attention to "a voice that is paradoxically released

through the wound" (2–3). She reads this scene as an illustration of
the latency of trauma and the ethical address delivered through
this belated knowing. A troubling aspect of Caruth's analysis is that
in its drive to identify Tancred as a trauma survivor, it tends to
obscure the wound inflicted on Clorinda. While Caruth cannot get
round the fact that it is Clorinda's voice that cries out from the
wound ("the wound that speaks is not precisely Tancred's own but
the wound, the trauma, of another" [8]), for her reading to work
she has to interpret Clorinda's voice as not exactly her own but as
(also) that of the traumatized Tancred's dissociated second self (Leys
295–96): Clorinda (also) represents "the other within the self that
retains the memory of the 'unwitting' traumatic events of one's past"
(Caruth, *Unclaimed Experience* 8). Caruth thus effectively rewrites the
wound inflicted on Clorinda as a trauma suffered by Tancred. Given
that this episode concerns the killing of an Ethiopian woman by
a European crusader, an orientalist dimension which Caruth does
not acknowledge,[3] her reading of this tale can be seen to illustrate
the difficulty of trauma theory to recognize the experience of the
non-Western other.[4]

I should add, though, that unlike Leys and Novak, who reject
the very suggestion that Tancred may have been traumatized by his
deed, I do not question Tancred's status as a survivor of (perpetrator)
trauma.[5] As Rothberg points out, Leys makes a "category error" by
"elid[ing] the category of 'victim' with that of the traumatized subject": "The categories of victim and perpetrator derive from either a
legal or a moral discourse, but the concept of trauma emerges from a
diagnostic realm that lies beyond guilt and innocence or good and
evil" (*Multidirectional Memory* 90).[6] Calling someone a trauma survivor or trauma victim does not in and of itself confer any moral capital on that person, as both victims and perpetrators can suffer trauma.
Nor do I share Leys's and Novak's tendency to identify Clorinda as the
real trauma victim in this case. To quote Rothberg once again, "The
dead are not traumatized, they are dead" (*Multidirectional Memory* 90).
What I do find problematic about Caruth's reading of this episode is
that Clorinda's experience is sidelined if not silenced altogether.[7]

This phenomenon is also noticeable in Caruth's interpretation
of Freud's speculative account of the origin of Judaism in *Moses
and Monotheism*, whose "central insight," according to Caruth, is
that "history, like trauma, is never simply one's own," that "history

is precisely the way we are implicated in each other's traumas" (*Unclaimed Experience* 24). She reads *Moses and Monotheism* as "the site of a trauma" (*Unclaimed Experience* 20): a product of Freud's own situation on the verge of the destruction of the European Jews by the Nazis, the text inscribes the author's personal trauma, Caruth argues, while also linking it to the history of Jewish monotheism, which Freud interprets as a history of trauma. In *Moses and Monotheism*, Freud attempts to explain Jewish history through the analogy of the effect of trauma on the individual. He postulates that the Jewish religion is founded on the slaying of Moses, an Egyptian nobleman who adhered to the monotheism of the pharaoh Akhenaten. After Moses led the Hebrews out of bondage in Egypt, Freud maintains, he was murdered by them in the wilderness out of resentment for the harsh laws he had tried to impose on them. Repressing the memory of the murder, the Hebrews reverted to polytheistic idol worship and took on a new leader, also called Moses, who was eventually assimilated to the original Moses. However, after a period of latency, the collective sense of patricidal guilt led to the return of the Mosaic law and the reaffirmation of Judaism as a monotheistic religion by way of atonement. Stressing the aporia of a history propelled by an inaccessible traumatic pre-history, which resonates with the way in which the structure of *Moses and Monotheism* bears witness to Freud's own experience of Nazi persecution, Caruth suggests that Freud's text urges us "to rethink the possibility of history, as well as our ethical and political relation to it" (*Unclaimed Experience* 12).

According to Leys, however, Caruth "decisively alters the terms of Freud's analysis" by positing the example of the railway accident rather than the child's Oedipal story as paradigmatic of Freud's treatment of the history of the Jews as the history of a trauma:

> Freud describes the experience of the Jews as a history of "what may properly be termed a traumatic experience" but which he characterizes as a murderous "crime" and the guilt-ridden return of the repressed. Caruth rejects Freud's castration model of the trauma in order to thematize the same story as the story of Jewish victimhood—as the history of a murder that, incredibly, "is not experienced [by the perpetrators] as it occurs," of an incomprehensible "missed" trauma that violently "separates" the Jews from Moses, of a traumatic "departure," a survival, and a literal

return—as if the Jews were victims and survivors of a completely unexpected, unintended, exogenous accident. (279–80)[8]

Leys discerns a pattern between Caruth's interpretation of the story of the murder of Moses and her reading of the story of Tancred and Clorinda: "Just as Caruth converts the Israelites who murdered Moses into passive victims of the trauma of an accidental 'separation,' so she converts Tancred into the victim of a trauma as well" (294). Unlike Leys, I do not question whether it is legitimate to consider perpetrators as trauma survivors. However, in this case too, I am troubled by the tendency to turn violence inflicted on a non-European other into a mere occasion for the exploration of the exemplary trauma suffered by the—in the terms of Freud's argument—European subjects responsible for that violence, which itself becomes obscured in the process. The Egyptian origins of Moses—duly noted by Caruth (*Unclaimed Experience* 13)—have received ample attention in recent years from scholars such as Jan Assmann (*Moses the Egyptian: The Memory of Egypt in Western Monotheism*, 1997) and Edward Said. In *Freud and the Non-European* (2003), for example, Said specifically focuses on Freud's provocative claim that the founder of Judaism was a non-Jewish Egyptian and its implication that Jewish identity, typically conceived as European, has a non-European aspect:

Let me return finally to Freud and his interest in the non-European as it bears on his attempt to reconstruct the primitive history of Jewish identity. What I find so compelling about it is that Freud seems to have made a special effort never to discount or play down the fact that Moses was non-European—especially since, in the terms of his argument, modern Judaism and the Jews were mainly to be thought of as European, or at least belonging to Europe rather than Asia or Africa. (50)

As with Tancred and Clorinda, then, an exemplary European trauma results from an act of violence against a non-European other whose true nature is concealed, in this case by the language of accident.

Also problematic, to my mind, is Caruth's discussion of *Hiroshima mon amour*, a film by Alain Resnais and Marguerite Duras which tells the story of a love affair between a Japanese architect and a French actress visiting Hiroshima to make a film about peace. In the film, the affair triggers a chain of memories as the woman relates the traumatic experiences she suffered at the end of the Second World War in the French city of Nevers. The young German soldier she had fallen in love with was shot and killed on the last day of fighting, just before they were to leave the city together. She was subsequently submitted to public disgrace, followed by a period of imprisonment and near-madness in her parents' home. Having recovered, she left home permanently, arriving in Paris on the day the war ended, after the bombing of Hiroshima and Nagasaki. It is her presence in Hiroshima, another site of wartime trauma, and the facilitating role of the Japanese man, who lost his family in the bombing, that enables the woman to recount her story for the first time. According to Caruth, the film demonstrates her thesis that trauma can act as a bridge between cultures: it allegedly opens up "a new mode of seeing and of listening" to the spectators, "a seeing and a listening *from the site of trauma*," which it offers as "the very possibility, in a catastrophic era, of a link between cultures" (*Unclaimed Experience* 56). This interpretation seems to me to gloss over the lop-sided quality of the cross-cultural dialogue established in *Hiroshima mon amour*. After all, we only ever get to hear the French woman's story; the traumatic history of Hiroshima in general or of the Japanese man in particular remains largely untold. Hiroshima is reduced to a stage on which the drama of a European woman's struggle to come to terms with her personal trauma can be played out; the Japanese man is of interest primarily as a catalyst and facilitator of this process. Caruth notes in passing that the film "does not tell the story of Hiroshima in 1945 but rather uses the rebuilt Hiroshima as the setting for the telling of another story, the French woman's story of Nevers" (*Unclaimed Experience* 27), but the asymmetry of the exchange and the appropriation and instrumentalization of Japanese suffering in the service of articulating a European trauma do not stop her from holding up the interaction between the French woman and the Japanese man as an exemplary model of cross-cultural witnessing.[9]

Nor is she discomforted by the fact that the connection that is established in the film between the collective memory of atomic destruction and the—historically less significant—personal tragedy of a *femme tondue* would appear to magnify the latter and downplay or eclipse the former. As Nancy Wood points out in *Vectors of Memory: Legacies of Trauma in Postwar Europe* (1999), the film's "recourse to analogy" generates unease in many viewers: "The discomfort that the film is still capable of provoking arises from the kinds of analogy it constructs between the personal memories of *une femme tondue*—women whose heads were shaven for (literally) 'sleeping with the enemy'—and the collective commemoration of an atomic conflagration" (185). In a footnote, though, Caruth argues that "the question of comparison" which made *Hiroshima mon amour* controversial has been "displaced or rethought" by the film (*Unclaimed Experience* 124n.14). As she points out, it is not possible to speak of comparison "in any simple sense" in relation to traumatic experiences: such partially unassimilated or missed experiences cannot be identified or equated, as this presupposes that they have been or can be "phenomenally perceived or made available to cognition" (*Unclaimed Experience* 124n.14). I am sympathetic to this argument—which I come back to at the end of Chapter 7—and I would not go so far as to claim that mass catastrophe and individual loss are simply equated with or analogized to one another. However, it seems to me that this does not invalidate the unease that many viewers feel about the vast difference in scale—unmeasurable though it may be—between the traumas that are linked together in *Hiroshima mon amour*.

Furthermore, Kalí Tal has accused Caruth of exoticizing the Japanese actor by taking for granted his alleged unawareness of the meaning of the lines he says in French, a language he did not know and had to learn to speak phonetically. According to Tal, such a complete detachment from meaning is highly unlikely if not impossible, and would never be claimed for a European actor finding himself in the same situation. Overstating her case, she concludes that "Caruth's own tendency to exoticize the Japanese, to believe in the alien quality of the Asian actor, leads her to unquestioningly embrace an ethnocentric and racist perspective" ("Remembering Difference").

What these examples show is that breaking with Eurocentrism requires a commitment not only to broadening the usual focus of trauma theory but also to acknowledging the traumas of non-Western or minority populations for their own sake. In the next chapter, I will argue that the traumas of non-Western or minority groups must be acknowledged, moreover, on their own terms. This, it seems to me, is another area where trauma theory has tended to fall short.

2
The Empire of Trauma

A product of history

Today the concept of trauma is widely used to describe responses to extreme events across space and time, as well as to guide their treatment. However, as Allan Young reminds us in *The Harmony of Illusions: Inventing Post-Traumatic Stress Disorder* (1995), it is actually a Western artefact, "invented" in the late nineteenth century: "The disorder is not timeless, nor does it possess an intrinsic unity. Rather, it is glued together by the practices, technologies, and narratives with which it is diagnosed, studied, treated, and represented and by the various interests, institutions, and moral arguments that mobilized these efforts and resources" (5). Similarly, in the introduction to *Traumatic Pasts: History, Psychiatry, and Trauma in the Modern Age, 1870–1930* (2001), Paul Lerner and Mark Micale note that their volume—an edited collection providing a historical study of the concept of trauma—"calls into question the idea of a single, uniform, transhistorically valid concept of psychological trauma by demonstrating its cultural and social contingence through a series of historical case studies" (25). The origins of this "historical product" (A. Young 5) can be located in a variety of medical and psychological discourses dealing with Euro-American experiences of industrialization, gender relations, and modern warfare (Micale and Lerner, eds.; Saunders; Saunders and Aghaie). As Laura Brown observes, hegemonic definitions of trauma have been constructed from the experiences of dominant groups in the West, that is, "white, young, able-bodied, educated, middle-class, Christian men" ("Not Outside the Range" 101). As a result, trauma has come to be understood as "that which disrupts these particular human lives, but no other" ("Not Outside the Range" 101).

The far-reaching implications of the fact that trauma is rooted in a particular historical and geographical context have long been ignored by academic researchers, including activist scholars fighting for public recognition of the psychic suffering inflicted on the socially disadvantaged. As Claire Stocks notes, the latter typically argue that the distress experienced by the constituencies whose cause they champion—for example, victims of sexual or racial abuse—is equivalent to experiences that are generally accepted as being traumatic, such as exposure to war-related violence (75–76). The feminist trauma theorist Judith Herman, for example, insists that her book *Trauma and Recovery: The Aftermath of Violence—from Domestic Abuse to Political Terror* (1992) is about "commonalities: between rape survivors and combat veterans, between battered women and political prisoners, between the survivors of vast concentration camps created by tyrants who rule nations and the survivors of small, hidden concentration camps created by tyrants who rule their homes" (3). She is concerned to "develop concepts that apply equally" to the experiences of these various groups (4). In *Worlds of Hurt: Reading the Literatures of Trauma* (1996), Kalí Tal, another feminist trauma theorist, similarly highlights parallels and correspondences between traumatic experiences suffered by men and women in very different situations and contexts. For example, she maintains that "the combat veteran of the Vietnam War responds viscerally to the transformed signs used by the survivor of the concentration camp since they mirror his or her own traumatic experience" (16), and that "[a]ll American women are threatened with violence, regardless of their race or class, just as all Jews were in danger in Nazi Germany" (20). This pervasive focus on similarity or sameness stems from a desire to gain recognition for the hitherto disregarded or overlooked suffering endured by disempowered groups. Noble as this goal is, such an approach risks erasing important differences and thereby ultimately doing more harm than good. It takes for granted rather than interrogates hegemonic definitions of trauma which are not scientifically neutral but culturally specific, and which will have to be revised and modified if they are to adequately account for—rather than to (re)colonize—the psychological pain inflicted on the downtrodden.

Indeed, it can be argued that the uncritical cross-cultural application of psychological concepts developed in the West amounts to a form of cultural imperialism. This claim has been made most forcefully by Derek Summerfield, a psychiatrist who sharply criticizes humanitarian interventions to provide psychological assistance in international conflict situations. "Psychiatric universalism," he writes, "risks being imperialistic, reminding us of the colonial era when what was presented to indigenous peoples was that there were different types of knowledge, and theirs was second-rate" ("Cross-Cultural Perspectives" 238). In the assumption that Western-style trauma programmes are necessary to avoid a postwar crop of psychiatric disorders, which is used as a basis for interventions in the lives of war-torn populations around the world, Summerfield hears "a modern echo of the age of Empire, when Christian missionaries set sail to cool the savagery of primitive peoples and gather their souls, which would otherwise be 'lost'" ("Critique" 1457).[1]

These and similar accusations are reiterated by Ethan Watters in his book *Crazy Like Us: The Globalization of the American Psyche* (2010).[2] Watters critiques what he calls "the grand project of Americanizing the world's understanding of the human mind" (*Crazy Like Us* 1). Over the past three decades, he writes, Americans have exported their ideas about mental health and illness around the world without regard for cultural differences, imposing their definitions and treatments as the international standards: "Indigenous forms of mental illness and healing are being bulldozed by disease categories and treatments made in the USA" (*Crazy Like Us* 3). One of the four case studies Watters examines is post-traumatic stress disorder (PTSD; the others are anorexia, schizophrenia, and depression). He reports on the Western trauma counsellors who arrived in Sri Lanka following the 2004 tsunami and who, in their rush to help the victims, inadvertently trampled local expressions of grief, suffering, and healing, thereby actually causing the community more distress.

The idea that Sri Lankans lacked local resources for psychological healing ignored or discounted the cultural traditions, beliefs, and rituals on which these people—who had lived through a 30-year civil war—relied. The resilience displayed by many Sri Lankans in the wake of the tsunami was seen as evidence that they were "in denial" and needed to be forced to confront the traumatic event that they had just experienced lest the unprocessed memory of it would begin to fester and manifest itself as PTSD. To that end the Western trauma counsellors employed a "debriefing" technique, which consisted of making the survivors retell or rework the traumatic event they had witnessed verbally or otherwise so as to allow them to process or master their traumatic memories. Watters argues that applying this approach—whose scientific validity he questions in any context—to post-tsunami Sri Lanka was ineffective and even harmful. He suggests that the remarkable psychological resilience shown by the Sri Lankan population, its capacity to live in the face of horror, can be partly accounted for by protective beliefs in Hindu and Buddhist traditions, such as an active acceptance of pain and suffering or the belief in rebirth and recompense through reincarnation (*Crazy Like Us* 89). Moreover, he claims that the central tenet of Western trauma counselling—that traumatic experiences must be retold and mastered—undermines local coping strategies, designed to keep the violence of the civil war from spiralling out of control, according to which the best way of dealing with trauma and containing the violence is not to talk about it directly (*Crazy Like Us* 107–14). Watters also points out that Sri Lankans tended to see the negative consequences of the tsunami not so much in terms of psychological damage as in terms of damage to social relationships (*Crazy Like Us* 91–93). "In a culture such as Sri Lanka's," therefore, "an emphasis on healing the individual away from the group, particularly in one-on-one counseling with strangers, is problematic" (*Crazy Like Us* 93).

As is well known, trauma gained official disease status in 1980, when it was included in the third edition of the authoritative *Diagnostic and Statistical Manual of Mental Disorders* (DSM) of the American Psychiatric Association as PTSD, a discrete and independent diagnostic entity appearing under the larger rubric of anxiety disorders. PTSD has been redefined in each subsequent version of the DSM, and is set to undergo further changes in the fifth edition, expected in 2013. That PTSD is widely believed to constitute a timeless, acultural, psychobiological phenomenon can be inferred from the fact that it is set apart from the "Culture-Bound Syndromes" described in a very short section far back in the DSM, that is, mental illnesses peculiar to certain cultures.[3] As Watters points out, "Western mental health practitioners are prone to believe that, unlike those culturally contrived manifestations of mental illness, the 844 pages of the *DSM-IV* prior to the inclusion of culture-bound syndromes describe *real* disorders of the mind, illnesses with symptomatology and outcomes relatively unaffected by shifting cultural beliefs. And, the logic goes, if they are unaffected by culture, then these disorders are surely universal to humans everywhere" (*Crazy Like Us* 5). However, many clinicians and researchers have come to feel that the PTSD construct reflects a Eurocentric, monocultural orientation (Spanierman and Poteat 521).[4] In a recent book, Brown calls what she describes as the "disconnection between the fields of trauma studies and cultural competence" both "surprising and ironic," as many of the early proponents of PTSD were social justice activists, involved in movements against the Vietnam War or for women's equality: "It might have been reasonable to assume that these socially conscious professionals, already deeply attuned to some forms of social injustice, would have looked next to issues of racism, classism, heterosexism, and other forms of oppressive inequality as they tried to enhance their comprehension of how trauma affected human lives; but that never occurred" (*Cultural Competence* 8).

Trauma and the everyday

Much criticism has been levelled at the DSM formulation of PTSD for its perceived failures of inclusiveness. Particularly contentious is Criterion A, the definition of what constitutes a traumatic stressor. According to the 1980 definition, PTSD is caused by an event that "would evoke significant symptoms of distress in most people" (DSM-III 238). Qualifying stressors, such as rape, military combat, earthquakes, aeroplane crashes, or torture, were those deemed to be "generally outside the range of usual human experience" (DSM-III 236). The revised 1987 edition expanded Criterion A to include witnessing or learning about one's family or friends being exposed to serious dangers as well as being directly exposed to such dangers oneself (DSM-III-R 250). The fourth edition, published in 1994, gives the following definition, which appears unchanged in the latest DSM version, a text revision of DSM-IV from 2000 called DSM-IV-TR:

> A. The person has been exposed to a traumatic event in which both of the following were present:
> (1) the person experienced, witnessed, or was confronted with an event or events that involved actual or threatened death or serious injury, or a threat to the physical integrity of self or others

(2) the person's response involved intense fear, helplessness, or horror. Note: In children, this may be expressed instead by disorganized or agitated behavior

(DSM-IV 427–28; DSM-IV-TR 467)

Note that the direct victim of the event is now no longer required to be among the family or friends of the witness, as was still the case in the DSM-III-R. The fact that Criterion A has broadened with almost each successive version of the DSM has led some critics to complain about "a conceptual bracket creep" (McNally 5) or "criterion creep" (Rosen et al. 4) in the definition of trauma. However, the preliminary draft revision of the DSM published on 10 February 2010 suggests that this trend will be reversed in the DSM-5, as the definition of what counts as a traumatic stressor has been "tighten[ed] up" so as "to make a better distinction between 'traumatic' [sic] and events that are distressing but which do not exceed the 'traumatic' threshold" (American Psychiatric Association, "Rationale"). Yet, many feminist and multicultural clinicians and researchers have argued that even in its current formulation Criterion A, though broad, is still narrow enough to make some important sources of trauma invisible and unknowable. In particular, it tends to ignore "the normative, quotidian aspects of trauma in the lives of many oppressed and disempowered persons, leading psychotherapists to an inability to grasp how a particular presentation of client distress is in fact posttraumatic" (L. Brown, *Cultural Competence* 18). The narrow range of possible traumas in people's lives implied by Criterion A needs to be expanded, it is argued, as there are many other experiences than those involving "actual or threatened death or serious injury, or a threat to the physical integrity of self or others" that can result in post-traumatic symptoms.

Concrete suggestions that have been offered for extending current definitions of trauma include type II traumas (Terr), complex PTSD or disorders of extreme stress not otherwise specified (Herman, "Complex PTSD"), safe-world violations (Janoff-Bulman), insidious trauma (Root), oppression-based trauma (Spanierman and Poteat), postcolonial syndrome (Duran et al.), postcolonial traumatic stress disorder (Turia), and post-traumatic slavery syndrome (Poussaint and Alexander). These attempts to go beyond or diversify the DSM definition of trauma can assist in understanding the impact of everyday racism, sexism, homophobia, classism, ableism, and other forms of structural oppression. Even though post-traumatic symptoms may be exhibited, the chronic psychic suffering caused by such experiences does not qualify for the PTSD diagnosis if, as is most often the case, an overt threat or act of violence is absent.

To give an example, I will briefly discuss racism as a source of what Maria Root calls "insidious trauma." In most Western countries, overt racism has largely been replaced with more covert, subtle, ambiguous, and complex racist incidents operating at institutional and cultural levels. Racism nowadays typically takes the form of daily micro-aggressions such as being denied promotions, home mortgages, or business loans; being a target of a security guard; being stopped in traffic; or seeing one's group portrayed in a stereotypical manner in the media. Unlike, say, hate crimes committed by an overtly racist perpetrator, such incidents involve no direct threat to life or physical safety and, as a result, do not fit the Criterion A definition of traumatic stressors.[5] One such incident alone may not be traumatizing, but traumatization can result insidiously from cumulative micro-aggressions: each one is too small to be a traumatic stressor, but together they can build to create an intense traumatic impact. As Jill Matus points out, "To claim that racial oppression should be viewed as productive of trauma is to move away from the emphasis on an overwhelming event that cannot be registered or recorded by the usual processes of memory in order to look at the local, habitual, everyday (therefore often unremarkable or invisible) forms of oppression" (29).

Thema Bryant-Davis and Carlota Ocampo list five barriers which, in their view, prevent the acknowledgement of racism as a source of trauma. The first of these barriers—the narrow DSM definition of trauma—can be regarded as a consequence of the other four. One of these is "moral disengagement": "If we deny the existence and impact of trauma, then we are relieved from the duty of having to respond to it" (405). This corresponds to the reason Brown gives to explain why, despite its activist roots, the field of trauma research has largely ignored issues of racism, heterosexism, classism, etc. According to Brown, it comes down to a matter of "'aversive' bias" (*Cultural Competence* 9), a form of bias that is denied by and is invisible to its practitioners. Questioning assumptions taken as truth by the dominant culture is threatening and induces shame in members of dominant groups: "The critical analysis of systemic forms of oppression requires those in positions of dominance and privilege, such as psychologists and other psychotherapists, to acknowledge the social locations of greater power stemming from their professional training and status and to see themselves as benefiting from oppression through the privilege inherent in those roles, whether or not they actively oppress others" (*Cultural Competence* 9). It is much more comfortable for mental health professionals to see themselves as neutral but caring bystanders, as "good people who, because they are not intentionally perpetrating oppression, are thus not involved in it nor necessarily responsible for its alleviation through the mechanism of their work" (*Cultural Competence* 9). Bryant-Davis and Ocampo also point to "the belief that broadening the category will demote the status of legitimate victims by diluting the definition of trauma" (485). They call the underlying premise that sympathy and resources are limited "destructive," and ask which gatekeeper will determine who the real victims are (485). Just as PTSD, which initially included only the experience of war veterans, was expanded through advocacy to include survivors of domestic violence and sexual assault, so ethnic minorities and their allies must now advocate for the recognition of racist-incident-based trauma as a legitimate traumatic experience, without in any way threatening the legitimacy of victims of other traumas (485). The fourth barrier which Bryant-Davis and Ocampo identify is the fear that broadening the trauma category will increase the financial accountability of perpetrators, leading to reparation lawsuits and compensation claims (485–86). The fifth and final barrier is the survivors' concern with being pathologized, as normal responses to traumatic incidents are categorized as disordered (486). Gwen Bergner concurs that "the potential to pathologize blackness" is "[n]o doubt the greatest danger in discussing the psychic effects of racism" (223).[6] Bryant-Davis and Ocampo point out, though, that the survivor should not be stigmatized, as it is the racist incidents that are the problem and the root of the disorder. Indeed, these alternative paradigms for comprehending traumatic stress precisely shift the blame from the individual victim to the social context by making visible the *en masse* oppression of target groups, whose continued existence it is emotionally and economically easier for society at large to deny.[7]

Dominant conceptions of trauma have often been criticized for considering trauma as an individual phenomenon and distracting attention from the wider social situation, which can be particularly problematic in a cross-cultural context (Wessells 269–71; Summerfield, "Critique" 1453–55). After all, in collectivist societies individualistic approaches may be at odds with the local culture. Moreover, by narrowly focusing on the level of the individual psyche, one tends to leave unquestioned the conditions that enabled the traumatic abuse, such as political oppression, racism, or economic domination. Problems that are essentially political, social, or economic are medicalized, and the people affected by them are pathologized as victims without agency, sufferers from an illness that can be cured through psychological counselling. The failure to situate these problems in their larger historical context can thus lead to psychological recovery being privileged over the transformation of a wounding political, social, or economic system. Insofar as it negates the need for taking collective action towards systemic change, the hegemonic trauma discourse can be seen to serve as a political palliative to the socially disempowered. Summerfield even goes so far as to suggest a continuity between the reframing of political, social, or economic phenomena as psychopathology by humanitarian disaster relief agencies today and the use of psychoanalytic concepts to characterize the restiveness of the colonized or the desire for freedom of the enslaved as the result of deficiencies in psychological structure and balance in a previous era. "Humanitarian interventions," he writes, "are not exempt from considerations of power and ideology, and may be at risk of an unwitting perpetuation of the colonial status of the non-Western mind" ("Critique" 1458).[8]

Pioneering postcolonial trauma theory

These criticisms of the individualizing, psychologizing, pathologizing, and depoliticizing tendencies of the dominant trauma model were anticipated by Frantz Fanon in his pioneering work on the psychopathology of racism and colonialism, especially in *Black Skin, White Masks* (1967 [1952]) and the last chapter of *The Wretched of the Earth* (1963 [1961]). As Rebecca Saunders notes, "Though rarely read as a trauma theorist, Frantz Fanon draws attention to crucial, yet often overlooked, episodes in the history of trauma: to the specific forms of trauma produced by colonial wars, by colonization itself, and, more diffusely, by racism" (13).[9] In "Colonial War and Mental

Disorders," the final chapter of *The Wretched of the Earth*, which follows the text's more famous sections on violence and national culture, Fanon describes the mental distress that colonial violence produces in both Algerians and their French colonizers through a series of psychiatric case studies of patients under his care. As he sets out to address "the problem of mental disorders born out of the national war of liberation waged by the Algerian people" (181), he observes that it is not just the war but also the colonial situation which it seeks to end that causes psychological damage: "The truth is that colonization, in its very essence, [before the war] already appeared to be a great purveyor of psychiatric hospitals" (181). In order to understand this, Fanon goes on, "we need only to study and appreciate the scope and depth of the wounds inflicted on the colonized during a single day under a colonial regime" (182). Even "[i]n the calm of this period of triumphant colonization," he argues, "a constant and considerable stream of mental symptoms are direct sequels of this oppression" (182).

Fanon's discussion of the psychological impact of colonialism in *The Wretched of the Earth* extends his analysis of the effects of racism in *Black Skin, White Masks*. A classic example of insidious trauma due to systematic oppression and discrimination is provided by his oft-cited account of encountering racial fear in a white child.[10] In "The Fact of Blackness," Chapter 5 of *Black Skin, White Masks*, Fanon describes how he felt his corporeal schema crumble as a result of being objectified as a demonic black figure in the eyes of a little white boy in Lyon, who, upon seeing him in the street, exclaimed: "Mama, look at the Negro! I'm frightened!" (112; trans. mod.). Associating the white child's fright with virulent expressions of racist hatred, Fanon recounts how the imposition of the child's gaze "abraded" his body "into nonbeing" (109). Stripped of his subjectivity, he became conscious of himself as "an object in the midst of other objects" (109). He compares the shock of encountering racial prejudice to psychic splitting—"I existed triply"—and physical amputation: "On that day, completely dislocated, unable to be abroad with the other, the white man, who unmercifully imprisoned me, I took myself far off from my own presence, far indeed, and made myself an object. What else could it be for me but an amputation, an excision, a hemorrhage that spattered my whole body with black blood?" (112). A little further on, Fanon tells us that "[m]y body was given back to me sprawled out, distorted, recolored, clad in mourning in that white winter day" (113). He speaks of "being dissected under white eyes," being *"fixed"* by those who "cut away slices of my reality" (116), and describes how "I felt knife blades open within me" (118). These persistent surgical metaphors, which recall the original, physiological meaning of trauma as a cut, lesion, or break in the body produced by an external force or agent, convey the devastating effect of contact with the objectifying and racializing gaze of the white European, which causes the black man to become alienated from himself. Fanon's analysis brings to light the harm done to marginalized groups by continuous exposure to "a galaxy of erosive stereotypes" (129), which leads them to develop feelings of inferiority, inadequacy, and self-hatred.

Moreover, Fanon calls attention to the social nature of the traumas caused by racial oppression, claiming, in *Black Skin, White Masks,* that "the black man's alienation is not an individual question" but, rather, "a question of a sociodiagnostic" (11). Hence, "the effective disalienation of the black man entails an immediate recognition of social and economic realities" (10–11). Fanon also questions the tendency of European psychoanalysis to focus exclusively on relations within the family unit and to assume a basic continuity between the family and the nation. A child growing up in a stable European family constellation later encounters a wider social world governed by the same values, rules, and principles. In the colonial situation, however, there is no such natural agreement between the family and the national culture. As Fanon points out, "A normal Negro child, having grown up within a normal family, will become abnormal on the slightest contact with the white world" (143). The discordance between the values, rules, and principles governing life in the family and those enforced in the social order makes the transition from childhood to adulthood a profoundly disorienting experience, and possibly a source of trauma, for the colonized. In another departure from traditional psychoanalysis, Fanon cautions against the inclination to value "the salvation of the soul" (11) over and at the expense of material liberation. The black man's chronically neurotic state of mind cannot be alleviated, he writes, as long as the socio-economic structure which brought it on remains unchanged: "There will be an authentic disalienation only to the degree to which things, in the most materialistic meaning of the word, will have been restored to their proper places" (11–12). As Françoise Vergès points out, for Fanon, "[i]ndividual alienation and political alienation are related; both are the product of social, political, and cultural conditions that must be transformed" (49).

Sticking to the event-based model

The concerns about the PTSD construct expressed by psychologists and other mental health professionals, and the alternative paradigms that they have proposed, have received very little attention from within the field of cultural trauma research. For the most part, cultural trauma theory remains oriented around the Freudian model that underlies and informs the psychiatric profession's official codification of trauma as PTSD (Wilson), taking no account of recent developments in psychological trauma research. Cultural trauma theory continues to adhere to the traditional event-based model of trauma, according to which trauma results from a single, extraordinary, catastrophic event. This is particularly noticeable in the work of Cathy Caruth and Dominick LaCapra, who engage more extensively and explicitly with psychological research on trauma than most other trauma theorists. Caruth mentions the debate about the introduction into the DSM of a category called disorders of extreme stress not otherwise specified (DESNOS) in the preface to *Trauma: Explorations in Memory* (viii) and includes an essay by Laura Brown criticizing the DSM definition of trauma in the same collection ("Not Outside the Range"), yet her work does not challenge the punctual trauma model which it takes as its starting point, and according to which "the accident" is "the exemplary scene of trauma *par excellence*" (*Unclaimed Experience* 6). This model also informs the neurobiological approach outlined in the essay by Bessel van der Kolk and Onno van der Hart in *Trauma: Explorations in Memory*, whose theory of the literal nature of traumatic memory fits well with Caruth's poststructuralist account (Leys 229–31): taking their cue from the work of Pierre Janet in particular, van der Kolk and van der Hart perpetuate the assumption that trauma is "a frightening event outside of ordinary human experience" (172).

The traumatic impact of racism and other forms of ongoing oppression cannot be adequately understood either in terms of the basic concepts and distinctions which LaCapra has introduced or expanded upon (Kennedy; Wilder), though bringing conceptual clarity to trauma theory is one of his most notable contributions to the field. One of LaCapra's key distinctions is that between loss and absence, which maps onto the distinction between historical and structural trauma. Loss "is situated on a historical level and is the consequence of particular events" (*Writing History* 64); absence, by contrast, is situated on "a transhistorical level" (*Writing History* 48), "is not an event and does not imply tenses (past, present, or future)" (*Writing History* 49), as it is a constitutive feature of existence— for example, the absence of ultimate foundations or metaphysical grounds (*Writing History* 50). Loss can be "worked through" (a concept LaCapra borrows from Freud); absence must be lived with. Useful as these distinctions are, it is hard to see how the trauma of racism fits into this picture. Unlike structural trauma, racism is historically specific; yet, unlike historical trauma, it is not related to a particular event, with a before and an after. Understanding racism as a historical trauma, which can be worked through, would be to obscure the fact that it continues to cause damage in the present. As Gary Wilder notes, "the idea of working through presupposes a normal distinction between past and present that has been unnaturally confused and needs to be restored. But what constitutes normal temporal distinctions when the structured past continues actively to structure the present?" (54).[11] Understanding racism in terms of structural trauma is no less problematic, though, as this would make it into a constitutive feature of existence, something that must be lived with.[12] As Rosanne Kennedy points out, "other concepts are needed" (104).[13] Moreover, as Victoria Burrows argues, this is a matter of some urgency: "until the daily occurrence of racial trauma becomes an important part of trauma theory, it will be addressing neither the structural nor the historical traumas of the twentieth century, nor will it provide a viable theoretical paradigm for the twenty-first" (18).

An article by Stocks that takes canonical trauma theory to task for its "cultural bias," which makes it "less applicable" to non-Western subjects (88), inadvertently shows how difficult it is for trauma theory to transcend this bias and to develop alternative conceptualizations attuned to racial and colonial trauma. Stocks denounces trauma theory's reliance on "specifically Western conceptions of the self" (73), according to which a psychologically healthy subject is unified, integrated, and whole, and questions the notion that healing from trauma consists of overcoming the fracturing of the self and the resulting division in identity caused by an extremely disturbing event. Stocks is right to point out that the assumption of "the pre-existence of a state of perceived psychic unity, which 'healing' aims to restore" (74), is often unwarranted: after all, for many disempowered groups, as we have seen, trauma is a constant presence, "a continuing background noise rather than an unusual event" (L. Brown, "Not Outside the Range" 103), meaning that there is no pre-traumatized state of being that can be restored in any straightforward manner. Unlike those (typically Western) subjects who have a sense of their own history as "ordinarily uninterrupted and coherent," "[t]hose for whom history is characterised by division may find it impossible or inappropriate to organise their memories in a singular, chronological fashion. Consequently, the kind of catharsis supposedly offered by the traditional 'talking cure' would presumably be unattainable since there is no single linear narrative into which to integrate traumatic memories" (Stocks 88). However, instead of challenging the one-size-fits-all application of the event-based model of trauma on the grounds that it risks ignoring the traumatizing effects of everyday oppression, Stocks surprisingly calls for a positive valorization of division, fragmentation, and multiplicity, which she conceives of as "a healthy or desirable foundation for the formation of identity" (75). Invoking the concept of "double consciousness," coined by W. E. B. Du Bois in *The Souls of Black Folk* (1990 [1903]) to describe the fractured psyche of black Americans, she expresses her regret that "the trauma theorists are inherently unable to reconcile multiplicity with mental health," even though she finds herself forced to admit that "the divided self may not be entirely unproblematical" (86). Indeed, Tal has fittingly called Du Bois's double consciousness "a graphic and apt descriptor of the effects of traumatic stress on an oppressed population" ("Remembering Difference"), effects which Stocks's approach carelessly embraces rather than interpreting them as signs of the traumatic impact of subjugation on the socially devalued.

Tainted origins

I would like to maintain, however, that trauma theory is not irremediably infused with Eurocentric bias, though such accusations have often been levelled at the main methodologies—psychoanalysis and deconstruction—from which it takes its inspiration. As Alfred López notes, psychoanalysis has come under attack by contemporary theorists of race, gender, and culture such as Gayatri Spivak and Jacques Derrida,[14] yet he believes that it remains "ideally suited to a theory and praxis of trauma, and colonial and postcolonial trauma in particular" (155). He keeps faith in the possibility of "a postcolonial psychoanalysis," that is, "a discourse that would learn to listen to its others and their needs, rather than impose upon those others universalized dogmas and schematics inherited from an often oppressive and violently dominating Western scientific and philosophical tradition" (173). He calls on psychoanalysis to "check its own tendencies toward universalization, and its complicities with the systematic imposition of Western cultural paradigms on the rest of the world that still poses as a universal humanism," and to respect heterogeneity and difference in dealing with the symptomatologies of cultures during and after empire (173).

In the same vein, Christopher Lane argues, in the introduction to *The Psychoanalysis of Race* (1998), that, despite its "tarnished" origins (13), psychoanalysis has much to teach us about race and racism. He defines the two aims of his collection as follows: "to ruin the myth that psychic enigmas are best explained as racial conflicts, and to critique the assumption that conflicts over the cultural meaning of race can be resolved *without* our tackling or understanding the unconscious" (20). On the one hand, assuming, with Freud and Carl Jung, that the unconscious operates as a "primitive" or "savage" constituency (13) would be to reproduce "egregious stereotypes about racial difference" (20); on the other, treating the unconscious as unimportant would be to misunderstand the "ongoing difficulty" of cross-racial harmony (20).

Ranjana Khanna's project in *Dark Continents: Psychoanalysis and Colonialism* (2003) is similar to López's and Lane's in that she, too, recognizes that psychoanalysis is "a colonial discipline" (x), yet refuses "to throw out the proverbial or indeed parochial baby with the bath water of political and economic colonialism" (28). Khanna acknowledges that psychoanalysis "brought into the world an idea of being that was dependent on colonial political and ontological relations, and through its disciplinary practices, formalized and perpetuated an idea of uncivilized, primitive, concealed, and timeless colonized peoples" (6). However, psychoanalysis is not doomed to assist in the repression of the colonized, but can be refashioned and reconfigured to become "the means through which contingent postcolonial futures can be imagined ethically" (xii). According to Khanna, psychoanalysis can be salvaged for postcolonial critique by being put through a process of "parochialization" or "provincialization." She sums up her argument as follows: "Far from rejecting psychoanalysis, *Dark Continents* shows the importance of psychoanalysis in the world today as a reading practice that makes apparent the psychical strife of colonial and postcolonial modernity. I argue that psychoanalysis itself is a colonial discipline, and that, as such, it provides mechanisms for the critique of postcoloniality and neocolonialism" (x).

Deconstruction, in its turn, like poststructuralism in general, has been accused of being irrelevant if not indifferent or even inimical to postcolonial concerns because of its alleged textualist bias and its location in the Western academy. These accusations have been levelled most famously by materialist critics such as Aijaz Ahmad, Benita Parry, and Neil Lazarus, who denounce the perceived depoliticization of postcolonial studies as theorized and practised by "culturalists" like Homi Bhabha and Spivak. Ahmad, for example, rejects the "apocalyptic anti-Marxism" supposedly espoused by postcolonial discourse, which he sees as the progeny of postmodernism, a catch-all phrase of derision for him that encapsulates poststructuralism and deconstruction (10). According to Ahmad, postcolonial critics such as Bhabha and Spivak, who take their inspiration from Derridean deconstruction, "subscribe to the idea of the end of Marxism, nationalism, collective historical subjects and revolutionary possibility as such" (10). Lazarus similarly denounces what he calls "the idealist and dehistoricizing scholarship" dominant in the field of postcolonial studies, and, like Ahmad, calls for a materialist critique (1). Parry also laments the rise of a postcolonial theory informed by poststructuralism, which, in her view, has shifted the focus away from politics and the violence of history:

The abandonment of historical and social explanation was soon apparent in the work of those postcolonial critics who disengaged colonialism from historical capitalism and re-presented it for study as a cultural event. Consequently an air-borne will to power was privileged over calculated compulsions, "discursive violence" took precedence over the practices of a violent system, and the intrinsically antagonistic colonial encounter was reconfigured as one of dialogue, complicity and transculturation. (4)

Postcolonial theory as conceived by Bhabha and Spivak is seen to mystify imperialism and to deny the agency and voice of the colonized.

According to other commentators, though, poststructuralism and deconstruction have made a valuable and positive contribution to postcolonial thought, which Ahmad, Lazarus, and Parry largely fail to acknowledge.[15] Stephen Morton, for example, while conceding that a postcolonial theory that is "too centred on the critique of the sovereign subject, the deconstruction of western metaphysics and the claim that all collective political resistance to imperialism is recuperated within a dominant system of power and knowledge" runs the risk of "denying the efficacy of collective political action, and the persistence of imperialism under the guise of neo-liberal globalization," stresses that poststructuralism is a crucial resource for effecting cultural and intellectual decolonization: "While poststructuralism was never explicitly aligned with the anti-colonial liberation thought of Frantz Fanon, the formulation of poststructuralism was nonetheless a product of decolonization in post-war France, and has provided some of the most influential postcolonial theorists, such as Homi K. Bhabha and Gayatri Spivak, with a set of conceptual tools to challenge the cultural and philosophical legacies of colonialism" (172).

The most robust defence of postcolonial theory's reliance on poststructuralism and deconstruction has been mounted by Robert Young in his books *White Mythologies: Writing History and the West* (1990) and *Postcolonialism: An Historical Introduction* (2001).[16] Young contends that poststructuralism originated not in May 1968, as is often claimed,[17] but in the Algerian War of Independence, and hence was always already postcolonial (*White Mythologies* 1). As he points out, many pioneers and key theorists of poststructuralism—Derrida, Hélène Cixous, Jean-François Lyotard, Louis Althusser, and Jean-Paul Sartre, among others—came from Algeria or were personally involved in the events of the war. Even though poststructuralism was taken up and developed in Europe, it was actually of non-European origin. Young goes so far as to suggest that the poststructuralism associated with these names can be characterized as "Franco-Maghrebian theory"; after all, he writes, "its theoretical interventions have been actively concerned with the task of undoing the ideological heritage of French colonialism and with rethinking the premises, assumptions and protocols of its centrist, imperial culture" (*Postcolonialism* 414). Young credits this poststructuralism born out of the experience of colonialism with having provided postcolonial studies with a critical vocabulary for challenging the systems of knowledge that support Western imperialism. He sees deconstruction in particular as part of an attempt to decolonize the forms of European thought: "If one had to answer... the general question of what is deconstruction a deconstruction of, the answer would be, of the concept, the authority, and assumed primacy of, the category of 'the West'" (*White Mythologies* 19). The critique of Western systems of knowledge that deconstruction offers is a vital step in the process of overturning the imperial order which those systems reflect and legitimate.

Coming down firmly on the side of those critics who argue that neither psychoanalysis nor deconstruction are fatally compromised by their (supposed) European provenance, I believe that trauma theory—as a product of their marriage—need not be abandoned altogether but can and should be reshaped, resituated, and redirected so as to foster attunement to previously unheard suffering.

3
Beyond Trauma Aesthetics

I have argued that trauma theory needs to become more inclusive and culturally sensitive by acknowledging the sufferings of non-Western and minority groups more fully, for their own sake, and on their own terms. In this chapter, I will address the textual inscription of such experiences and suggest that certain received ideas and assumptions about how literature bears witness to trauma may need to be revised. The title of this chapter is adapted from a book by Rita Felski called *Beyond Feminist Aesthetics: Feminist Literature and Social Change* (1989), which is more than 20 years old now but whose argument remains pertinent and can help us understand what is wrong with trauma aesthetics. Felski contends that it is impossible to construct a normative aesthetic for feminist literature.[1] This "chimera" has hindered attempts to adequately assess the merits and shortcomings of contemporary feminist writing, she argues, "by measuring it against an abstract conception of a 'feminine' writing practice, which in recent years has been most frequently derived from an antirealist aesthetics of textuality" (2). Felski specifically has in mind then-current approaches in French feminist literary theory which privileged avant-garde experimental writing that challenges conventional modes of representation, approaches which—as Toril Moi had noted in her highly influential book *Sexual/Textual Politics: Feminist Literary Theory* (1985)—appeared to have superseded "content-based" Anglo-American feminist literary theory, with its preference for accessible, realist writing reflecting women's experience. Felski seeks to dispel the notion that there is a uniquely or specifically feminine style of writing, and that literary forms can be classified along gender lines. The question of the most suitable and effective strategy for a feminist writing practice cannot be settled a priori without taking into account the social and historical contexts in which literature is written and read:

> it is impossible to speak of "masculine" and "feminine" in any meaningful sense in the formal analysis of texts; the political value of literary texts from the standpoint of feminism can be determined only by an investigation of their social functions and effects in relation to the interests of women in a particular historical context, and not by attempting to deduce an abstract literary theory of "masculine" and "feminine," "subversive" and "reactionary" forms in isolation from the social conditions of their production and reception. (1–2)

Hence, Felski herself uses the term "feminist literature" as a descriptive rather than a prescriptive category, a label which is "intended to embrace the diversity of contemporary literary texts which engage sympathetically with feminist ideas, whatever their particular form" (12). In what follows, I will put forward an analogous argument in relation to trauma literature: drawing on important work by Jill Bennett and Rosanne Kennedy (their edited volume *World Memory*) and by Roger Luckhurst (a monograph titled *The Trauma Question* [2008]), I will challenge the notion, which has become all but axiomatic within trauma theory, that traumatic experiences can only be adequately represented through the use of experimental, modernist textual strategies.

Modernist attachments

This preference for avant-garde or modernist forms can be traced back to Theodor Adorno's notorious pronouncements about poetry after Auschwitz, which marked the beginning of the debate about whether and how to represent the Holocaust. In his essay "Cultural Criticism and Society," written in 1949 and published in 1951, Adorno famously states: "It is barbaric to write a poem after Auschwitz, and that is why it has become impossible to write poetry today" (31). He revisited this much-cited verdict against representation in his essay "Commitment," published in 1962. In this later essay,

Adorno clarifies that what he specifically objected to was "the aesthetic principle of stylization" (312), which transforms the fate of
the victims in such a way as to remove its horror. Insofar as it mobi-
lizes suffering for the enjoyment of the reader or the spectator, art
does an injustice to the victims. Adorno reiterates his earlier claim—
"I have no wish to soften the saying that to write lyric poetry after
Auschwitz is barbaric"—but goes on to complicate or even contradict
it by adding that "literature must resist this verdict" as "[i]t is now
virtually in art alone that suffering can still find its own voice, conso-
lation, without immediately being betrayed by it" (312). His primary
example of a morally acceptable post-Auschwitz aesthetic is the art
of Samuel Beckett, which allegedly evades the problem of pleasure
through its refusal of realist figuration.[2] Adorno's marked predilec-
tion for "autonomous" art, which avoids realism and is characterized
by fragmentation and aporia, appears to be shared by most trauma
theorists—one can think, for example, of Shoshana Felman's readings of Paul Celan's poetry and Claude Lanzmann's film *Shoah*, or
Cathy Caruth's analysis of *Hiroshima mon amour*.

  However, given "the wealth of Holocaust representations over the
decades," Andreas Huyssen confesses his increasing scepticism about
(Adorno-inspired) "demands that on principle posit an aesthetics
and an ethics of nonrepresentability," which, as he points out, is
"itself an ideology" ("Resistance to Memory" 169). This aesthetic
amounts to "a last-ditch defense of modernist purity against the
onslaught of new and old forms of representation," and its ethics
risks becoming mere "moralizing against any form of representation
that does not meet the assumed standard" ("Resistance to Memory"
169). The result, Huyssen notes, is "a Holocaust formalism that all
too often draws on the old distinction between art and mass media,
high and low culture" ("Resistance to Memory" 169). This preference for a formalist aesthetic is arguably even more problematic in
the field of trauma theory, whose object of study in principle if
not in practice—is much more diverse than (representations of) a
single historical catastrophe. At the same time, though, the attachment to modernism appears to be more deeply ingrained: as Bennett
and Kennedy observe, trauma theorists often justify their focus on
anti-narrative, fragmented, modernist forms by pointing to similarities with the psychic experience of trauma (9–10). An experience
that exceeds the possibility of narrative knowledge, so the logic goes,

will best be represented by a failure of narrative. Hence, what is called for is the disruption of conventional modes of representation, such as can be found in modernist art. As Luckhurst puts it, "fractured Modernist form mimics narrative possibility disarmed by trauma" (81).

This assumption, which is "surprisingly prescriptive," could lead to the establishment of a narrow trauma canon consisting of non-linear, modernist texts by mostly Western writers, modernism being a European cultural tradition: "there is a danger that the field is becoming limited to a selection of texts that represent a relatively narrow range of traumatic events, histories and cultural forms, rather than engaging the global scope of traumatic events and the myriad forms that bear witness to them" (Bennett and Kennedy 10). Bennett and Kennedy go on to deplore the tendency to select texts for study on the basis of how well they illustrate prevailing theories of trauma rather than because they provide insight into a wide range of traumatic events and histories and into the variety of forms that representations of trauma take (10). Luckhurst also laments trauma theory's sole focus on anti-narrative texts and points out that the crisis of representation caused by trauma generates narrative *possibility* just as much as narrative *impossibility*. Beyond the narrow canon of high-brow, avant-garde texts, he reminds us, "a wide diversity of high, middle and low cultural forms have provided a repertoire of compelling ways to articulate that apparently paradoxical thing, the trauma narrative" (83). In his book, Luckhurst explores this broad range of testimonial forms, studying popular trauma memoirs and novels—by Stephen King, for example—alongside canonical trauma texts.

Positioning the reader

Apart from sharing certain formal features, the kinds of testimonial texts favoured by most trauma theorists also tend to address and position the reader in a particular way. In an essay on Stolen Generation testimonies included in *World Memory*, Kennedy and Tikka Jan Wilson show how in testimony as theorized by Felman and Dori Laub the relationship between the witness and the reader is based on that between the analysand and the analyst in the psychoanalytic situation. The respective subject positions into which the witness and the reader are interpellated are those of a passive, inarticulate victim on the one hand and a knowledgeable expert on the other. The former bears witness to a truth of which he or she is not fully conscious, and can do so only indirectly, making it impossible for his or her testimony to act as a political intervention. The latter responds to the witness's testimony by showing empathy and vicariously experiencing his or her trauma, a reaction which supposedly obviates any need for critical self-reflection regarding his or her own implication in ongoing practices of oppression and denial.[3] There is no place in this model for testimony in which the narrator speaks as an expert about his or her own experience, making political claims and actively intervening into power relations.

A good example of this kind of testimony are the vernacular Stolen Generation testimonies which Kennedy and Wilson look at, in which the narrator—an Aborigine who was removed from his or her family as a child by the Australian government to be brought up in an institution or fostered out to a white family—does not ask the reader, who is addressed as a white Australian, for empathy but to become critically conscious of his or her own role in the ongoing conspiracy of silence regarding Aboriginal history and Aboriginal dispossession. The reader is addressed here not as an innocent victim but as a bystander or potential collaborator. As Amy Novak and Robert Eaglestone have shown, the same is true for much recent trauma literature coming out of Africa or concerning Africa addressed to a Western audience, for example, Ishmael Beah's memoir *A Long Way Gone: Memoirs of a Boy Soldier* (2007), Uzodinma Iweala's novel *Beasts of No Nation* (2005), Dave Eggers's fictionalized memoir *What Is the What: The Autobiography of Valentino Achak Deng* (2006), Chimamanda Ngozi Adichie's novel *Half of a Yellow Sun* (2006), and Christopher Abani's novel *GraceLand* (2004). Rather than inviting the reader to become a vicarious victim, these texts denounce and fight the indifference of a privileged and empowered Western public to the suffering of the racial, ethnic, or cultural other. The sense of political urgency informing these texts may go some way towards explaining their reliance on a no-frills, realist aesthetic, which sets them apart from the emergent canon of trauma literature: the overriding concern is to get the message across and to mobilize. Eaglestone remarks on the "burning political need" driving much Western-facing African trauma literature: "As in Holocaust narrative, there is a sense that the story must be told. But perhaps here there is also a more burning political need. As the news daily reminds us, ... many of these sorts of events are continuing. Without anyone grasping them, perhaps nothing can be done. These works are 'engaged literature' in a renewed Sartrean sense; that is, they are not simply affective works: they are also aimed explicitly at pricking Western consciences" (82).

Dismissing such literature out of hand for failing to conform to a particular aesthetic found and valued in a relatively small body of mostly Western high-brow works of art seems to me to be misguided, patronizing, and damaging to the ethical ideals to which trauma theory aspires. This does not mean that I reject modernist modes of representation as inherently Eurocentric, nor that I advocate realism or indigenous literary forms as a postcolonial panacea. However, I do think it is important to check the rush to dismiss whatever deviates from the prescribed aesthetic as regressive or irrelevant. As Huyssen argues in relation to Holocaust formalism, it is preferable to analyse "how representations in different aesthetic and narrative modes and in different media have shaped processes of public memory and forgetting in different countries and cultures" and to acknowledge "the changing conditions of mediation and transmission that may require new forms, new genres, and new media for public memory to renew itself" ("Resistance to Memory" 169). Rather than positing a necessary relation between aesthetic form and political or ethical effectiveness, trauma theory should take account of the specific social and historical contexts in which trauma narratives are produced and received, and be open and attentive to the diverse strategies of representation and resistance which these contexts invite or necessitate.

4

Ordinary Trauma in Sindiwe Magona's *Mother to Mother*

Considered in terms of a struggle over definitions of trauma and recovery, the work of the South African Truth and Reconciliation Commission (TRC), the criticisms levelled against it, and the literary response it has evoked shed an interesting light on the debate over the monocultural bias of trauma theory in its "classical," mid-1990s formulation and the fraught relationship between such tendencies and the commitment to social justice on which the field prides itself. In *Writing History, Writing Trauma*, Dominick LaCapra reflects that the TRC "was in its own way a trauma recovery center" (43). The TRC attempted to uncover the truth about the gross human rights violations committed during apartheid and to promote national unity and reconciliation through a collective process of working through the past. Insofar as the TRC mapped Euro-American concepts of trauma and recovery onto an apartheid-colonial situation, it was subject to the same problems and limitations faced by trauma theory—problems and limitations which post-apartheid literature has not been slow to confront. The novelist André Brink has famously declared that "unless the enquiries of the Truth and Reconciliation Commission (TRC) are extended, complicated, and intensified in the imaginings of literature, society cannot sufficiently come to terms with its past to face the future" (30). Sindiwe Magona's truth-and-reconciliation novel *Mother to Mother* (1999 [1998]) assumes just this task: it can be seen to supplement the work of the TRC by critically revisiting its limits, exclusions, and elisions—and thus also to suggest a possible way for "traditional" trauma theory to reinvent and renew itself.

The TRC and the persistence of the past

Many of the objections raised to the uncritical export of Euro-American models of trauma and recovery bear a close resemblance to criticisms which have been levelled at the TRC. It, too, has been accused of downplaying, individualizing, pathologizing, and depoliticizing the lived experience of subjection. For example, Mahmood Mamdani has noted that the TRC's decision to individualize the victims of apartheid sits uneasily with its formal acknowledgement of apartheid as a "crime against humanity" which systematically discriminated and dehumanized entire communities:[1] "If the 'crime against humanity' involved a targeting of entire communities for racial and ethnic cleansing and policing, individualizing the victim obliterated this particular—many would argue *central*—characteristic of apartheid" ("Amnesty" 34). By defining as victims only "those whose rights had been violated through acts of killing, torture, abduction and severe ill treatment" (*TRC Report*, vol. 1, ch. 4, par. 53), the TRC failed to adequately address the injustices of apartheid as a legalized system of oppression which had blighted the everyday lives of many millions of South Africans. Mamdani claims that the TRC displayed "a systematic lack of interest in the crime which was institutionalised as the law" and was "interested only in violations outside the law" ("Reconciliation" 3). To bring to light the truth about apartheid, it would have had to "put centre-stage the experience of apartheid as a banal reality" ("Reconciliation" 4). Mamdani's criticism of the TRC clearly resonates with our observation that the current trauma discourse has difficulty recognizing that it is not just singular and extraordinary events but also "normal," everyday humiliations and abuses that can act as traumatic stressors.

The TRC's pursuit of reconciliation has proved no less contentious than the modalities of its truth-finding mission. Its deployment of therapeutic and theological ideas of healing and redemption in the service of an explicit nation-building agenda led to accusations that the TRC attempted to impose premature closure on the past. The TRC did in fact emphasize the cathartic role of victim testimony and the closure it must bring: "We open wounds only in order to cleanse them, to deal with the past effectively and so to close the door on that dark and horrendous past forever" (*TRC Interim Report* 1). In his foreword to the TRC's final report, chairman Desmond

Tutu similarly recommended "shut[ting] the door on the past" or "clos[ing] the chapter on our past" once we—South Africans—had "looked the beast of the past in the eye," "asked and received forgiveness," and "made amends," so that we could "move into the glorious future of a new kind of society" unencumbered by past wounds (vol. 1, ch. 1, par. 91, 93). Christopher Colvin has drawn attention to the opposition by victims of apartheid-era violence to the therapeutic ethic informing the work of the TRC: "For the members of the [Khulumani Victim Support] group, their key assertion is that things have not changed and that to ask victims to tell their stories of (and thus recover from) *prior* suffering for the good of the nation is premature, insulting and politically suspect" (164). These members feel as if they are being asked to do the hard work of retrieving and recounting painful memories for the benefit of others. While their testimony is used to reconcile and redeem the South African nation, their own suffering—which is only partly due to the acutely traumatizing events about which they testified—remains largely unalleviated. Colvin quotes one victim as saying: "It does no good. . . . I tell my story to the TRC, I tell it to the Trauma Centre and still I have nothing. I am so frustrated. Why do they want to know my story if they don't do anything for me, they give me nothing except, oh, we are so sorry, Mrs. H . . . no, I will not tell my story again. They are just laughing at me" (165). In another interview, Mrs H voices her suspicion that the only purpose which her testimony served was to help ease the conscience of bleeding-heart liberals, for whom providing psychological support to victims of apartheid represents an attractive alternative to the kind of real socio-economic and material change that would see them lose their privileged status: "They [Trauma Centre facilitators] just want us to be victims and tell our stories so they can help us. I am sick of telling my story. It makes them feel good to show that they are helping us, that things are really OK. They don't really want to change things and what good does telling our stories over and over and over do?" (165).[2]

Mrs H gives eloquent expression to the sense of anger and frustration felt by many witnesses at the perceived depoliticization of their testimony. Allen Feldman reminds us that this was hardly the intent of the TRC, and that it would be misguided to simply dismiss the TRC as a politically naive exercise in therapeutic uplift: "The popular and media-generated view that the TRC hearings were planned and conducted by weepy psychotherapists was far from reality." According to Feldman, TRC staff were well aware that the talking cure is no panacea: "Truth telling and fact setting were seen as correctives to the apartheid era's official mendacity, historical falsification, and clandestine counterinsurgency, but not as activities that would mechanically bring resolution, comity, or conciliation." They were under no illusion that holding hearings, letting people talk, and publishing reports would automatically bring about social healing; in their thinking, this goal was "intimately tied to social movement notions of disability rights, societal integration, and economic empowerment." The survivors of human rights abuses who testified before the TRC perceived themselves, and were perceived by the commission, as political actors:

> Many witnesses rejected the biographical nomination of "victim," with all the passive and depoliticizing connotations this term implies, choosing instead the term "survivor," which allows for a sense of political agency. Submitting testimony was not therefore seen as wounded persons showing their scars in public, but rather as an act of political and historical intervention: setting the record straight after the systemic mendacity and disinformation of the former regime.

However, as Feldman points out, the TRC's tendency to see recollection as "inherently beneficial"—because of its need for data and because the act of recall so effectively counterbalanced the repression of memory under apartheid—"could easily slip into a metaphysics of the talking cure." According to Feldman, the TRC did in fact end up "stressing memory's therapeutic possibilities at the expense of establishing its pathogenic connection to institutional violence and that violence's inherence in economic racism." This was *a fortiori* the case with subsequent representations of the TRC in media, human rights, and other discourses, which reduced its proceedings to "a ceremony of cathartic trauma exposure" and "rewrote the complex story of the research and the hearings in terms of the transnational cultural intelligibility of trauma narratives and confessional talking cures."

There are, of course, pragmatic reasons why the TRC focused on individuals involved in specific acts and on psychological recovery rather than on the wholesale degradation of millions of people and on material recovery. The kind of exacting political critique of the power dynamics at work in society called for by the latter approach would have seriously complicated the achievement of the objective of reconciliation, which was strongly foregrounded in the TRC process, as demanded by the compromise legislation which created the TRC and set the limits of its work (that is, the "Promotion of National Unity and Reconciliation Act" of 1995). Psychological healing and interpersonal reconciliation seeming easier to deliver in the short term than their material and political counterparts, it made pragmatic sense from a government point of view for the TRC to stress the former dimension at the expense of the latter as a way of playing for time. As Giuliana Lund observes, "the pacifying nature of the discourse of healing and reconciliation may be productive to the extent that it helps maintain peace in the land, reassures foreign investors, and keeps the economy running, all important for the long-term welfare of the people" (113).

However, there is a thin line between helping along the inevitably slow process of improving the material living conditions of the majority population by staving off social unrest, and bolstering the status quo by bending over backwards not to alienate white South Africans or international capital. Quite a few commentators are of the opinion that the latter is what has actually happened. Yazir Henri and Heidi Grunebaum, for example, express their disillusionment with the outcome of the TRC process, which, they argue, "nurtured...the possibility for those who benefited and continue to benefit from colonial and Apartheid rule to consolidate socio-economic relations of power informed by direct socio-economic structuring based on previously legally defined 'race' categories" (2). Little has changed when the peace bought by the TRC "translates as the wholesale suffering of the majority of Black South Africans and the continued protection of 'white' privilege and benefit whilst colonial and Enlightenment histories of destruction in the name of progress and civilisation are gradually cast into obscurity" (2).

Mother to Mother as a literary response to the TRC

In this section, I will analyse the inscription of traumatic memory in Sindiwe Magona's novel *Mother to Mother*, which seems to me to be a particularly relevant literary response to the TRC as a trauma recovery project. Published in 1998, *Mother to Mother* is a fictional-ized account of the Amy Biehl killing which can be seen to negotiate the different conceptions of trauma elaborated above. Amy Biehl was a young white American Fulbright scholar and anti-apartheid activist who had come to South Africa to assist in the process of prepar-ing the country's first non-racial democratic election. On the day before her scheduled return to the United States in 1993, her vehi-cle was attacked as she was driving friends home in the township of Guguletu, and she was stoned and stabbed to death by four black youths who were returning from a meeting of the Pan Africanist Students' Organisation (PASO) where militant slogans such as "One settler, one bullet" had been chanted. The murder of Amy Biehl brought an overwhelming public outpouring of grief and outrage, and received considerable media attention at the time. When the four killers, who had been convicted and sentenced to 18 years each, later applied to the TRC for amnesty, Amy's parents surprised many by not opposing the application. In July 1997 the four testified before the amnesty committee of the TRC, and amnesty was granted to all of them in August 1998. Peter and Linda Biehl also met with the family of Mongezi Christopher Manqina, one of their daughter's murderers, after Mongezi's mother had sent Linda Biehl a message expressing sorrow at her son's responsibility for Amy's death. These dramatic events were not only widely reported in the media but also documented in *Long Night's Journey into Day*, an award-winning doc-umentary film which follows four high-profile cases brought before the TRC. The Biehls went on to set up the Amy Biehl Foundation, a non-profit organization dedicated to community development in the townships of Cape Town. Remarkably, this charitable foundation, which honours the memory of their daughter, employs two of the youths involved in her death.

Magona, who grew up in Guguletu herself but was then living in New York, learnt eight months after Amy's murder that Mongezi's mother was her childhood friend Evelyn Manqina, a discovery which moved her for the first time to empathize with the killers' fami-lies. She started writing *Mother to Mother* in 1996, the year in which the TRC began its hearings, and the book came out in the year in which the TRC concluded its work and presented its report. Looking beyond the book's production history, we find that its close associa-tion with the TRC is also borne out by its thematic preoccupations.

In the "Author's Preface" Magona explains that her aim in writing the book was to describe not the world of the victim, which had been much talked about already, but "the other world," that of the perpetrators, which had attracted far less interest:

> And yet, are there no lessons to be had from knowing something of the other world? The reverse of such benevolent and nurturing entities as those that throw up the Amy Biehls, the Andrew Goodmans, and other young people of that quality? What was the world of this young women's [sic] killers, the world of those, young as she was young, whose environment failed to nurture them in the higher ideals of humanity and who, instead, became lost creatures of malice and destruction? (v)

In addition to drawing attention to the world of the perpetrators, *Mother to Mother* also seeks to bring the two worlds into contact. The novel retells the events of the day of the murder and the day after to Linda Biehl in the voice of the fictional Mandisa, the mother of Amy's killer Mxolisi, a character based on Mongezi Manqina (in Magona's novel there is only one murderer). Mandisa never actually names the victim or her mother, referring to them throughout the narrative as "your daughter" and "you," but the "Author's Preface" leaves the reader in no doubt as to their identity. Moreover, the close resemblance between Mandisa's own name and that of the author, of which it is a semi-anagram (*Sind*iwe *Magon*a), suggests a deep affinity between the protagonist and her creator. Rather than locking herself up in her own world of pain, Mandisa evokes the connection between Linda Biehl and herself as mothers: "My Sister-Mother, we are bound in this sorrow" (201). While expressing her grief over Amy's death, Mandisa also asks for understanding for her son, from Linda Biehl but by extension also from the reader: "you have to understand my son" (1). Mandisa's narrative is a moving attempt to reach out and share grief, offer comfort, and foster mutual understanding across racial, ethnic, and cultural boundaries.

Before I go on to analyse the novel in some detail, let me point out that the bridge-building effort undertaken in *Mother to Mother* was anticipated by the short story "Two Little Girls and a City," which appeared in Magona's 1991 collection *Living, Loving, and Lying Awake at Night*. This story recounts the tragedy experienced by two mothers in Cape Town, one white and privileged, one black and poverty-stricken, whose young daughters are brutally raped and murdered in separate incidents—one in the affluent suburb of Sea Point, one "[e]ight miles away" (118) in the township of Guguletu—but on the same hot summer day. The text interweaves the two narrative strands, alternating segments describing different moments from the two girls' stories with one another. It thus suggests parallels between the suffering of the respective victims and their families, despite the vast differences of race and class that keep them apart. However, while the text testifies to a desire to bridge these divisions and to unite the mothers in their sorrow, the stories never actually come together at the plot level, as the two groups of characters do not interact with one another in any way. In fact, the narrator takes pains to emphasize the stark contrast between the worlds inhabited by the two girls, which are reminiscent of the two worlds of which Magona speaks in the "Author's Preface" to *Mother to Mother*. She bitterly notes that, whereas the death of the white girl—Nina van Niekerk— made front-page news in the *Cape Times*, the death of the black girl—Phumla Dyantyi—went unreported in the media. Moreover, while the police and the church are shown to be eminently supportive of the relatives of the white girl, the family of the black girl receives little or no assistance from these institutions. Furthermore, even though the identity of the perpetrator(s) is unknown, and remains so throughout the narrative, suspicion immediately falls on the black community. Many of its members are rudely questioned by the police, leading to anger and resentment. The story ends as follows:

> Today, no one knows the name of the little girl found in a rubbish drum at the back of the butcher's shop [Phumla Dyantyi]. They don't know it today, for they never knew it then.
> ...Since the story never made the news, most never knew her name....And yet, not a few remember the name Nina van Niekerk. In Guguletu. After all these years...more than ten.
> They remember the sorrow. The grief of mothers. The murder of innocent little girls. In Cape Town. They remember the horror. And, to this day they still wonder, how they found themselves foremost among suspects. Great sorrow. And burning anger. (141–42)

The same ingredients—differential treatment of blacks and whites, burning anger, horror, and the grief of mothers—are also to be found in *Mother to Mother*, which further develops themes first broached in "Two Little Girls and a City."

An important point which Mandisa seeks to drive home, and which could be viewed as an implicit criticism of the TRC, is that a proper understanding of Mxolisi's murderous act requires a full appreciation of the traumatizing impact of apartheid on the people it reduced to second-class citizens. As Magona has said in a recent interview with Karin Orantes, "white South Africans still do not understand what it meant to live under apartheid on the receiving end of that stick" (qtd. in Orantes 32); they do not sufficiently realize "who we are, how we've been scarred, I mean the psychic wounding of people who grew up knowing that there is no hope in hell of ever escaping their plight" (qtd. in Orantes 33). *Mother to Mother* shows that it will not do to consider sudden eruptions of violence such as the one that resulted in the death of Amy Biehl in isolation from the larger context in which they occur and which, indeed, produces them. Mandisa's memories of the week of 25 August 1993, the date of Amy's murder, are interwoven with flashbacks which illuminate the rest of her and her son's lives. She describes her family's forced removal from the semi-urban village of Blouvlei under the notorious Group Areas Act and the subsequent break-up of the Blouvlei community; her unwelcome teenage pregnancy and its dire consequences, including denial of schooling and entrapment in domestic servitude; the misery, hardship, and bleakness of township life; the constant threat and reality of police brutality; and the ubiquity of intra-ethnic violence. As Meg Samuelson points out, the focus of Mandisa's memories is on the "everyday": "Mandisa's story becomes a liturgy of the 'ordinary' violence inflicted on her by *both* the apartheid state and local patriarchies" (*Remembering* 166). As her story unfolds, the reader comes to share Mandisa's lack of surprise at Mxolisi's act, which she repeatedly emphasizes: "Let me say out plain, I was not surprised that my son killed your daughter" (1); "Nothing my son does surprises me any more" (88). After all, but for the skin colour of the victim, this murder was hardly an unusual event in Guguletu: "For years…many, many years, we have lived with violence. This was nothing new to us. What was new was that this time, the victim was white" (69).

The novel depicts one such violent incident in particular, as it had a devastating impact on Mxolisi during his childhood. Pursued by the police after attending a political rally, two of Mxolisi's older friends hide themselves in a wardrobe in their parents' house. The police are about to leave, having been convinced by the family that the boys had escaped by jumping over the back fence, when the four-year-old Mxolisi, thinking that this is just a game of hide-and-seek, shouts out his friends' location. As the boys try to flee, they are shot dead by the police, in full view of the toddler, who is "struck mute" by what he has witnessed: "After that, he zipped his mouth and would not say one word. Not one word more—for the next two years" (148). In an article published in 1986, Frank Chicane confirms the traumatizing effect of pervasive state violence on children in the townships. He writes that the conditions under which township children grow up "have affected children more than many people realize":

> The world of the township child is extremely violent. It is a world made up of teargas, bullets, whippings, detention, and death on the street. It is an experience of military operations and night raids, of roadblocks and body searches. It is a world where parents and friends get carried away in the night to be interrogated. It is a world where people simply disappear, where parents are assassinated and homes are petrol bombed. Such is the environment of the township child today. (342–43)

Indeed, for all its horror, the incident witnessed by Mxolisi is not an uncommon occurrence in Guguletu: in the world of the township, violence is the rule rather than the exception, the norm rather than the departure from it—quite the opposite, that is, of the ordinary way of the Biehls' world.[3] As Gill Straker points out in a 1987 article co-authored with the Sanctuaries Counselling Team, persecution and victimization are not "historical events" but "continuing common everyday practices" in the townships (76). She calls the term *post-traumatic stress syndrome* "a misnomer" in the South African context, as the inhabitants of the country's black townships are subjected to "*continuous* traumatic stress," occasioned by "the high levels of violence" encountered there (48). When Mandisa at one point speaks of "an ordinary day" in Guguletu, she immediately adds the following clarification: "ordinary, in the context of our lives that have become quite complex and far from ordinary" (73).

With this context in place, Mandisa represents the murder of Amy Biehl not as the senseless action of one atomized individual, but as "[t]he enactment of the deep, dark, private yearnings of a subjugated race" (210). Mxolisi, in this view, did not act autonomously but was only "an agent, executing the long-simmering dark desires of his race" (210). Just as she ascribes a wider representative role to Mxolisi, so Mandisa sees Amy as a stand-in for the white community in general, referring to her death as "the sacrifice of [her race]" (210). In fact, Mandisa's own story also signifies beyond itself, as the experiences she recounts resonate with the suffering of millions of black South Africans living under apartheid. As Magona states in the interview with Orantes, the story of the woman on whom the character of Mandisa is based is "the story of the people, the majority of us that I call perfect products of apartheid: someone who became what the apartheid government wanted all of us to become. Her potential was just never anywhere near being realized; it couldn't be, it was lost to apartheid. And she is like so many, the walking dead" (qtd. in Orantes 46).

The novel makes it clear that the dark desires acted upon by Mxolisi have been simmering for centuries rather than decades. The insidious traumas inflicted by apartheid and the violent reaction these provoked are connected with the "abomination" of colonialism and the Xhosa cattle-killing of 1856–1857 (178). These links are established in an episode in which Mandisa as a child is instructed by her grandfather about Nongqawuse's prophecy and the cattle-killing movement, which led to mass starvation and ushered in a new era of colonial expansion and domination. Mandisa's grandfather sets out to disabuse his granddaughter of the notion, implanted in her by her schoolteachers, that the Xhosa people lent the "false prophet" Nongqawuse a willing ear "[b]ecause they were superstitious and ignorant" (175). He points out that what had prompted the Xhosa nation's decision to burn all their fields and slaughter all their cattle was the hope that this radical measure would "drive *abelungu* [white people] to the sea, where, so the seer had said, they would all drown" (178). In his view, the extreme nature of the Xhosa people's actions testifies to the gravity of their suffering at the hands of the white colonizers and the depth of their resentment: "How deep the resentment to have spurred them to such terrible sacrifice. How deep the abomination, to trigger such a response" (178). The change in Mandisa's perspective on the cattle-killing incident which her grandfather's history lesson brings about mirrors that wished upon the addressee and the reader of Magona's book in regard to Amy Biehl's death: "Tatomkhulu was a fund of facts that, although seemingly different, made a whole lot of sense of some of the things we learned at school. He explained what had seemed stupid decisions, and acts that had seemed indefensible became not only understandable but highly honourable" (183). Thus, in addition to apartheid, the novel commemorates another history of destruction in the name of civilization which has been cast into obscurity, to repeat Henri and Grunebaum's words. This history is also invoked in the description of the harsh wind buffeting the Cape Flats to which the Blouvlei community has been relocated: "By night, it howled and wailed and shrieked like the despairing voices of lost souls. In fact, some said what we heard of nights were the voices of Malay slaves lost in a ship wrecked hereabouts, when the area was still all sea" (30). In this way, the forced removals under apartheid witnessed firsthand by Mandisa are associated with the early history of colonialism in the Cape. Moreover, by taking a long historical view and highlighting the continuity between the colonial and the apartheid era, the novel can be seen to question the wisdom of the TRC's exclusive focus on the period from 1960 to 1994.[4]

According to Mandisa, these centuries of trauma and oppression have produced a generation of children driven to savage behaviour, as the "Young Lions" of the resistance movement go around the townships murdering suspected informers or burning down their houses: "Our children fast descended into barbarism. With impunity, they broke with old tradition and crossed the boundary between that which separates human beings from beasts. Humaneness, *ubuntu*, took flight. It had been sorely violated. It went and buried itself where none of us would easily find it again" (76). As Shane Graham points out in relation to this passage, "The word *ubuntu* now inevitably evokes the TRC and Tutu's theology of restorative justice, but Mandisa's cynicism here implies that the quality of human compassion underlying this philosophy has been destroyed" (80). Indeed, apart from uncovering hidden histories of violence and oppression, *Mother to Mother* also critically reflects on the possibilities for healing and reconciliation in the wake of the traumas of colonialism and apartheid. The novel's invocation of biblical rhetoric, which recalls the TRC's religious underpinnings, at first seems to suggest confidence in the likelihood of a redemptive outcome. Not only is Amy's death discussed in terms of sacrifice and atonement for the sins of the white race (201; 210), but Mxolisi, who turns out to be the product of a virgin birth and whose name means "[h]e, who would bring peace" (136), is also portrayed as a Christ figure—despite being referred to as "[t]he perfect host of the demons of his [race]" at one point (201).[5] However, the hope of an end to the bloodshed and a new era of peace aroused by these religious overtones is dashed by Mandisa's stern warning that

> the same winds that gouged dongas in my son's soul are still blowing... blowing ever strong. There are three- and four-year-olds as well as other children, roaming the streets of Guguletu with nothing to do all day long. Those children, as true as the sun rises in the east and sets in the west—those young people are walking the same road my son walked. (199)

In other words, as long as there is no significant improvement in the material well-being of the black population, of which the novel paints such a grim picture, the cycle of violence will continue unabated. The storm, an image which is put to good use throughout the novel to evoke the centuries-old strife and turmoil caused by racial divisions in South Africa, shows no sign of dying down (Samuelson, "The Mother as Witness" 140–41). Offering a sobering assessment of the aftermath of the victory of the anti-apartheid struggle, *Mother to Mother* demands sustained scepticism regarding some of the illusions attaching to "Truth and Reconciliation" in the "new" South Africa.

Magona repeats this critique in the interview with Orantes. Asked for her thoughts on the work done by the TRC, she says that the TRC "did a lot of good" but failed to be "universal": "It was for a small pocket of people, the 'stars of apartheid' as I call them. For the ordinary men in the street it did absolutely nothing" (qtd. in Orantes 42). In the wake of apartheid, South Africa has contented itself with "doing a little patchwork here, patchwork there instead of systematic mending of the brokenness with which we came to our freedom.

We came to freedom in brokenness, and there has been no real going back and patching of the things that were broken, mending them, examining them" (qtd. in Orantes 43). Rather than addressing "what is radically wrong," going to the "root cause," the policies that were put in place were largely superficial and ineffective—Magona compares them to "putting salve on a cancer" (qtd. in Orantes 43). Pressed to elaborate, she explains that, by focusing on spectacular violent incidents, the TRC ignored the slow violence of structural oppression which led black South Africans to become politically active and put themselves in harm's way in the first place:

> It's good to say: "Your husband died, your child died in this way." But before these people died, there is a reason they were in that position of jeopardy. People didn't start suffering when they were on Robben Island. There is a reason they landed on Robben Island: their lives before Robben Island were lives of suffering, and that is the suffering of all black people, and that is the suffering that hasn't been addressed. It's as if people started suffering once they were arrested. They would not have been arrested if their lives had been cosy outside. They were arrested because they were protesting, fighting against an untenable situation, an inhuman situation: the way we lived. The way we lived, it's a miracle that so many of us survived.
>
> (qtd. in Orantes 44)

Magona attributes lethal force not only to the extra-legal actions of the security services, which directly affected a relatively small number of people, but also to "the way we lived"; that is, apartheid as an everyday reality which generated massive numbers of "walking dead." She fears for her country as long as the reality of material inequality inherited from apartheid, responsible for so many "wasted lives" (qtd. in Orantes 46), remains unchanged. As in *Mother to Mother*, she expresses her concern about the lack of opportunities available to black children in South Africa even today:

> We don't know what we do, how we destroy ourselves and how we do ourselves a disservice when we fail to nurture the littlest of our children. Children should be ours in community, and each nation should make sure that all its children are shepherded safely

through childhood to adulthood, so that they emerge from the
house of childhood fully functioning, self-respecting, law-abiding
members of society, so that they can make the contributions they
were meant to make.

(qtd. in Orantes 46)

While *Mother to Mother* calls for scepticism towards grandiose
proclamations of healing and reconciliation, it does so not in a spirit
of fatalism or despair,[6] but in the stubborn belief that there is hope
in crossing boundaries to witness the pain of others. In trying to
find words of grief to bridge worlds of grief, Magona's novel maintains faith in the idea that trauma provides the link between cultures,
and that working towards a fuller appreciation of the nature, extent,
and ramifications of the pain of others can, indeed, help efforts to
alleviate it. Still, it must be borne in mind that the addressee in
Mother to Mother is a white American, not a white South African.
As Samuelson notes, this raises the question of whether "this 'con-
versation' [would] have been possible for Magona if Biehl had been
a white South African" ("Reading" 234). Indeed, "[o]ne could query
the choice of this specific event as opposed to, for example, the similar story of Lindy-Anne [sic] Fourie, the white South African girl
killed in the Heidelberg Tavern massacre" ("Reading" 234). There are
indeed remarkable parallels between the stories of Amy Biehl and
Lyndi Fourie, who died in the same year in an attack on a Cape Town
restaurant carried out by the Azanian People's Liberation Army, the
armed wing of the Pan Africanist Congress, which left four people
dead. Like the Biehls, Lyndi's mother Ginn Fourie did not oppose the
killers' request for amnesty from the TRC. Moreover, in 2002 she for-
gave the man who had ordered the attack, Letlapa Mphahlele, and
together they set up the Lyndi Fourie Foundation, whose mission is
to further conciliation in South Africa.

Magona could have chosen to write about this all South African
case or imagined one like it, as Elleke Boehmer does in her 2002
novel *Bloodlines*, which is strikingly similar to *Mother to Mother* in
many respects (Gready 165–67).[7] Both novels are set during the transition period from apartheid to democracy in the early 1990s, and
thematize interpersonal reconciliation between the loved ones of a
white victim and a black perpetrator, who is clearly presented as himself a victim of apartheid. Just as Magona seeks to understand "the

other world," the world of the perpetrators, in *Mother to Mother*, so the protagonist of *Bloodlines*, the girlfriend of one of the victims of a bombing at a supermarket, is in search of "[a] story from the other side" (112), which is why she reaches out to the perpetrator's mother. Unlike Boehmer, however, Magona does not tell an all-South African reconciliation story but one in which the bereaved party is a white American woman. Samuelson detects a contradiction in *Mother to Mother* between "a wish to cross barriers" and "a lingering reluctance to make affiliations with white South African women" ("Reading" 234). While Magona identifies important weaknesses of the TRC and suggests ways of overcoming them, she appears unable or unwilling— as yet—to take on the task of imagining cross-racial alliances in South Africa. If, as I have argued, her novel heralds the establishment of a new, more inclusive and culturally sensitive kind of trauma theory, it also makes clear the long road that remains to be travelled.

5
Mid-Mourning in David Dabydeen's "Turner" and Fred D'Aguiar's *Feeding the Ghosts*

Just as Magona's novel can be read as a critique of the TRC's tendency—which it shares with trauma theory in its classical formulation—to map Western conceptions of trauma straightforwardly onto an apartheid-colonial situation, so the two literary works that I will look at next can be seen to challenge traditional understandings of trauma, mourning, and recovery that risk obscuring the continuing oppressive effects of racial trauma. David Dabydeen's epic poem "Turner" (2002 [1995]) and Fred D'Aguiar's novel *Feeding the Ghosts* (1998 [1997]) both memorialize the Middle Passage, a history that has come to epitomize the experience of people of African descent throughout the Atlantic world. Both texts resist the temptation to leave the reader with the sense that the story has been told, consigned to the past; that it has been taken care of and can therefore now be forgotten. Rather than affirming a clear distinction between the past and the present, they insist that racist attitudes and practices persist throughout the ages. Disrupting popular understandings of history as a linear progression from a colonial or slave past to a liberated "postcolonial" present, they invite an ethico-political practice of anamnestic solidarity with the oppressed of the past *and* the present. Taking my cue from Jacques Derrida's reflections on spectrality and mourning, I argue that "Turner" and *Feeding the Ghosts* open up a space of remembrance in which historical losses are neither introjected nor incorporated, neither "properly" mourned nor melancholically entombed within the self, but constantly re-examined and re-interpreted.

Hauntology and mid-mourning

In *Specters of Marx: The State of the Debt, the Work of Mourning, and the New International* (1994), the book which initiated the perceived "ethical turn" in his work, Derrida argues that the possibility of a just future depends on our readiness "to learn to live *with* ghosts" (xviii). He insists on an obligation to live not solely in the present but "beyond all living present," aware of and attentive to those already dead or not yet born. Being neither fully present nor fully absent, ghosts do not have a determinate ontological status but belong to a liminal "hauntological" domain which allows for an ongoing politics of memory and a concern for justice:

> No justice...seems possible or thinkable without the principle of some *responsibility*, beyond all living present, within that which disjoins the living present, before the ghosts of those who are not yet born or who are already dead, be they victims of wars, political or other kinds of violence, nationalist, racist, colonialist, sexist, or other kinds of exterminations, victims of the oppressions of capitalist imperialism or any of the forms of totalitarianism. (xix)

This responsibility involves facing up to what Derrida terms the "*non-contemporaneity of the living present*" (xix), the "disjointure in the very presence of the present," which makes it possible to "*think the ghost*" (25). As Derrida points out, traditional scholars do not believe in ghosts: they maintain an ontological perspective, drawing a sharp distinction between the living and the non-living, being and non-being, the past and the present (11). However, he anticipates the coming of "another 'scholar'" (12), "the 'scholar' of the future," who, unlike his or her predecessor, would be capable of "thinking the possibility of the specter" and of having commerce with the *revenants* and *arrivants* of history (176).

As is well known, Derrida launched this call for an ethico-political engagement with a present that is not ontologically fixated on "what is" in opposition to the end-of-history triumphalism of Francis Fukuyama, who argued that the end of the Cold War signalled the end of the progression of human history. Fukuyama envisaged the end of history as the universal incarnation of liberal democracy and the final eradication of the spectre of communism. Derrida, in contrast, insists on the continuing relevance of Karl Marx, or a certain spirit of Marx, to the world today, which, despite Fukuyama's protestations to the contrary, is really "going badly" (77): "never have violence, inequality, exclusion, famine, and thus economic oppression affected as many human beings in the history of the earth and of humanity.... no degree of progress allows one to ignore that never before, in absolute figures, never have so many men, women, and children been subjugated, starved, or exterminated on the earth" (85). He rejects Fukuyama's attempt to exorcize Marx's ghost and his refusal to inherit from him, assuming instead the necessity of an interminable mourning—which elsewhere he calls "demi-deuil," translated as "mid-mourning" ("Freud's Legacy" 335) or "semi-mourning" (*"Ja*, or the *faux-bond* II" 48), and which is to be distinguished from the traditional, Freudian understanding of mourning as a process involving the gradual withdrawal of libidinal attachment from a lost object (Freud, "Mourning and Melancholia"). As Alessia Ricciardi explains, mid-mourning differs from mourning in the Freudian sense in that it "does not pretend to achieve a successful 'dismissal' of the lost object, but instead adopts an inconclusive psychic rhythm of oscillation between introjection and incorporation" (36). The distinction between introjection and incorporation—which was developed by Nicolas Abraham and Maria Torok, and which the concept of mid-mourning unsettles—is analogous to Freud's distinction between mourning and melancholia: the former integrates loss into consciousness, assimilates and digests the other; the latter fails or refuses to do so, taking the other into the self as other. Mid-mourning hovers between the introjection of successful resolved mourning and the incorporation of pathological grieving or melancholia. It allows the subject to be "perpetually reexposed to history rather than removed from it" (Ricciardi 34), the latter being the inevitable result of both introjection and incorporation in their ideal, pure state. Introjection removes the subject from history by rendering the otherness of history entirely assimilable. Incorporation, for its part, while preserving this otherness, is really no more faithful to history than introjection, as it excludes the otherness of history from the self and prevents the subject from engaging with it (Derrida, "Fors" xvii, xxi–xxii). Mid-mourning, however, which keeps introjection and incorporation in a permanent state of tension, is a continual working-over of a history which remains enigmatic and irreducibly other.

Derrida's hauntological politics of memory can help counter the premature and obfuscatory celebration of the "post" in "postcolonial," a concept which has been the subject of criticism by Anne McClintock, Ella Shohat, Stuart Hall, and others. Insofar as it implies that colonialism is now a matter of the past and, therefore, over and done with, the postcolonial partakes of an apocalyptic discourse, a discourse on or of the end. However, the traumas sustained by the formerly colonized and enslaved are collective in nature and impossible to locate in an event that took place at a singular, historically specific moment in time. They are part of a long history of racism and exploitation that persists into the present. As Victoria Burrows argues, it is only if one disavows colonialism's traumatic legacies that one can declare it to be over:

> In terms of the colonial/postcolonial binary, the question of who gets to be fortunate enough to effect closure on historical traumas is bound up with the imagined dismantling of colonialism. There are ongoing traumas for many millions of peoples whose lives are still disproportionately circumscribed by the often intense suffering created by the changing face of power structures that have transmogrified into neo-colonialism, cultural imperialism and now the injustices (racial, gendered and classed) inherent in the universalistic notion of global capitalism. Only those who can ignore "the belated scar[s]"—both metaphorical and literal—inscribed on the lives of millions who *live the consequences* of colonialism can retreat, in the words of Robert Young, into the "safety of its politics of the past." (21)

Pointing out that "[t]he word *postcolonial* itself has embedded within it an unforgotten and unforgettable history: the impact of the colonial, that is to say, of empire" (18), Linda Hutcheon claims that "the witnessing of the trauma of colonization" is the central task of postcolonial literary studies (19). Hauntology, as a discourse on the end of the end which proceeds in the name of justice, can be of great epistemological as well as ethico-political value in this context. In what follows, I will try to illustrate this by examining the inscription of the trauma of the Middle Passage in "Turner" and

Feeding the Ghost.[1] Both texts bear literary witness to the *Zong* massacre of 1781, a true incident in which a British slave-ship captain murdered 132 sickly and allegedly dying Africans by throwing them over the side of the ship in order to be able to claim insurance money.[2] A chilling example of the horrors of the slave trade, the *Zong* massacre became a *cause célèbre* for eighteenth-century abolitionists, and in 1840 inspired J. M. W. Turner to paint his famous portrait of a ship jettisoning its human cargo during a violent storm, entitled *Slavers Throwing Overboard the Dead and Dying: Typhon [sic] Coming On* but better known as *The Slave Ship*. In their own way, Dabydeen's poem and D'Aguiar's novel both resist the temptation to leave the reader with the sense that the story has been told, consigned to the past; that it has been taken care of and can therefore now be forgotten. Instead of clearing away the dead, they permit this traumatic history to live on as a haunting, troubling, foreign element within the present.[3]

"Turner" and the oppressive weight of history

Dabydeen's "Turner" is a long narrative poem, divided into 25 sections, which gives a voice to the submerged African in the foreground of Turner's painting.[4] As is apparent from the preface, the poem is a response to John Ruskin's infamous description of Turner's picture in *Modern Painters*, which relegates the jettisoned slaves to a footnote—a footnote that, as Dabydeen puts it, "reads like an afterthought, something tossed overboard" (7). The speaker of the poem struggles to fabricate a new self and a new history, but remains trapped by the powerful forces of the past, which keeps resurfacing in the present. The sea, so the drowning slave claims, has transformed him: it has "bleached" (IX. 15) him of colour; washed his skin clean of "the colour of sin, scab, smudge,/Pestilence, death, rats that carry plague,/Darkness such as blots the sky when locusts swarm" (XI 20–22). However, his desire for newness is counterpointed by racist name-calling. The word "nigger" is hurled at him time and again by a stillborn child thrown overboard some time later:

> "Nigger," it cries, loosening from the hook
> Of my desire, drifting away from
> My body of lies. I wanted to teach it

A redemptive song, fashion new descriptions
Of things, new colours fountaining out of form.
I wanted to begin anew in the sea
But the child would not bear the future
Nor its inventions... (XXV. 1–8)

As Dabydeen suggests in the poem's preface, this child, which may be seen as the speaker's unconscious and origin, serves as an "agent of self-recognition" (8) in the poem. The child, "drowned as it is in the memory of ancient cruelty" (8), sees through "the sea's disguise" (XI. 18), "recognis[es] [him] below [his] skin" (XI. 19), making him realize that the stains left by a collective history of racial abuse cannot be washed away so easily. The recurrent scene of the child calling the speaker "nigger" and its effect on him are reminiscent of Frantz Fanon's famous account of encountering racial prejudice in a little white boy, which I discussed in Chapter 2: "'Dirty nigger!' Or simply, 'Look, a Negro!' I came into the world imbued with the will to find a meaning in things, my spirit filled with the desire to attain to the source of the world, and then I found that I was an object in the midst of other objects" (*Black Skin* 109).[5] Confronted with his body's representation within a history that denies his humanity, Fanon finds his own bodily experience altered: "Then, assailed at various points, the corporeal schema crumbled, its place taken by a racial epidermal schema" (*Black Skin* 112). Like that of the speaker of Dabydeen's poem, his body is exposed as a "body of lies" (XXV. 3) by this encounter, which makes him realize the crushing impact of centuries of racist exploitation and stereotyping: "I subjected myself to an objective examination, I discovered my blackness, my ethnic characteristics; and I was battered down by tom-toms, cannibalism, intellectual deficiency, fetishism [sic], racial defects, slave-ships, and above all else, above all: 'Sho' good eatin'" (*Black Skin* 112).

In "Turner," the oppressive weight of this history is apparent from the opening line, in which the child is described as "[s]tillborn from all the signs" (I. 1): the ubiquity of racializing and "othering" discourses destroys the promise of new life and a fresh start traditionally associated with birth imagery. While the speaker desired to "so shape/This creature's bone and cell and word beyond/Memory of obscene human form" (XVIII. 12–14), the child "made me heed its distress at being/Human and alive, its anger at my/Coaxing it awake" (XVIII. 15–17). It is a ghost which refuses to be transfigured and thereby consigned to oblivion—which, the poem suggests, would in fact amount to another violation, comparable to the slave-ship captain's paedophiliac acts: indeed, "the hook/of [the speaker's] desire" (XXV. 1–2) from which the child loosens itself in one of the excerpts quoted above recalls the captain's "hook/Implanted in our flesh" (XXIV. 10–11) from the previous section of the poem.[6] Like the spectres of which Derrida writes, the child continually recalls the speaker to the out-of-jointness of the present. In an interview, Dabydeen has spoken of his identification with the stillborn child of the poem, which, he says, was prompted by his own experience of contemporary racism:

> I mean, I feel as if I'm an abortion, at times. I feel like the stillborn child in "Turner", definitely. Or even worse than that, I feel like an abortion; messy and bloody and unborn, and that's partly because of a racism, where other people are trying to reduce you to nothing all the time and erase everything that you brought with you, or else they remind you of what you could have brought with you had they not taken it away.
>
> (qtd. in Dawes 219–20)

The stillborn child effectively frustrates the process of introjection to which the speaker has devoted himself for most of the poem. Indeed, in response to the child's indignant cries, he negates his entire imaginative creation in the final section of the text:

> No savannah, moon, gods, magicians
> To heal or curse, harvests, ceremonies,
> No men to plough, corn to fatten their herds,
> No stars, no land, no words, no community,
> No mother. (XXV. 38–42)

While the poem may seem to end on a pessimistic note,[7] its unmaking of itself need not be seen as purely negative: the text's refusal of an affirmative and redemptive ending can also be interpreted as a gesture of deference to, or a sign of sympathy with, the hauntological.[8]

Feeding the Ghosts and the unending voyage of the *Zong*

A confrontation between a wish for renewal and the indelible stains of history is also enacted in *Feeding the Ghosts*, a reconstruction of the *Zong* incident in prose form which centres on the experience of a fictional female slave, Mintah, who miraculously survives being cast overboard for her "insubordination" in questioning the jettisoning of sick slaves. The novel is divided into three main parts and framed by a prologue and an epilogue. The first and longest part recreates the tragedy from the perspective of different characters, including black slaves as well as white crew members. The second section is an account of the 1783 court case brought by the insurers, at which Mintah's written record of the events on board the *Zong* surfaces but is dismissed as a book "penned by a ghost" (169): as Abigail Ward points out, "Her status as 'ghost' renders her not quite real or believable" (160). The last section begins with Mintah's written account of the *Zong* and continues with her life in Maryland and Jamaica, haunted by memories of the *Zong*. The narrative ends in 1833, with Mintah, in her old age, observing the celebrations for the abolition of slavery in Jamaica. The novel sets out to commemorate the 131 victims of the *Zong* massacre, whose souls, as the prologue puts it, "roam the Atlantic with countless others" (4). Mintah, who acts as the novel's moral centre, dedicates her entire life after the *Zong* to keeping alive their memory, an occupation which the text refers to as "feeding the ghosts": "Ghosts needed to be fed. She carved and wrote to assuage their hunger" (222). Not only does she set her memories of the *Zong* down in writing and carve 131 figures out of wood, but she also plants 131 trees and helps twice as many slaves escape to freedom from Maryland to the North.

Despite all this commemorative activity, the history of the *Zong* remains fundamentally unresolved. The novel uses various means to drive this point home, including the well-worn device of the false ending, which is provided by Mintah's euphoric description of the abolition celebrations. Finding herself at the centre of the festivities, she recognizes the dancers in the square as the wooden figures she had carved, and realizes she has misread these all along:

> I thought the shapes were trying to rise from the sea, but now I know they were dances. Each figure made by me was in this

square. A man, woman or child in some movement to the music. Not movements to the music of the sea, as I had thought. These were dances of freedom. The faces were not scared on those figures but excited. I had made them then read them wrong. Now they were here before me showing me their meaning, and I had helped to shape it. They were dancing not struggling. Ecstatic not terrified. (218)

Mintah and the community appear to have successfully overcome the past, as her carvings are stripped of their traumatic meaning and as she is honoured by the community and finally even reunited with Simon, the one good white crew member of the *Zong*. However, at this point Mintah (and the reader with her) wakes from her dream— a fantasy of introjection—to find that in reality none of this is the case. The freedom celebrations come to ring hollow as in actual fact the community cannot "take what she had to say," "doubt[s] that the events had taken place" (223), and has no taste for her uncanny or "unhomely" sculptures: "They love what I do with wood but cannot keep such a shape in their homes. Such shapes do not quench a thirst. They unsettle a stomach. Fill the eyes with unease" (209).[9] The present can will the past away but cannot actually rid itself of its haunting power.

   That a truly new, unencumbered future cannot be born yet is also signalled by Mintah's infertility, a direct consequence of her experiences on the *Zong* ("The sea had taken my blood from me and my ability to bleed"), which prevents her from being "made into newer shapes of people" through reproduction (210). Her only progeny are the wooden figures, which represent and are inhabited by the ghosts of the uncared-for dead of the *Zong*. When at the end of the narrative proper Mintah's house burns down with everything in it, "[t]he spirits carved in those figures fled into the wooded hills" (226). The ghosts, in other words, are still at large by novel's end. The inconclusive ending—the real one, that is—thus belies the confidence expressed in the oft-quoted final sentence of the epilogue: "The past is laid to rest when it is told" (216).[10] So, in fact, does the very form of the novel, which, as Ian Baucom points out, is marked by a "melancholy reiterativity" (79). In each of the five sections of the text, the same events are told and retold. The novel "finds itself obliged to tell its tale not once but serially" (Baucom 77), as if it were condemned to an endless repetition compulsion. This is in keeping with the author's own claim, in his 1996 article "The Last Essay about Slavery," that there is a compulsive need to revisit slavery for every succeeding generation of black writers. Rather than it being the case that the past is laid to rest when it is told, D'Aguiar argues, "each articulation, each imagining, feeds the need for a further act of retrieval" (138). The fact that *Feeding the Ghosts* is already his second novel about slavery—after *The Longest Memory* (1994)—bears out the truth of this statement even in the context of D'Aguiar's own œuvre.

The epilogue reveals the reason why the *Zong* incident cannot be successfully mourned. A ghostly voice, belonging to a slave thrown overboard on the *Zong*, insists that this traumatic history resonates far beyond its original moment: "All the cruelties we sustained were maintained by us. Made over hundreds of years, our behaviour could never cease to exist.... That ship was in that sea and we were in it and that would be for an eternity in a voyage without beginning or end" (229). The case of the *Zong* is lifted out of time to suggest the persistence of racist attitudes and practices throughout the ages. The voice goes on to directly address the reader, implicating him or her in the events of 1781:

> I am in your community, in a cottage or apartment or cardboard box, tucked away in a quiet corner, ruminating over these very things. The *Zong* is on the high seas. Men, women and children are thrown overboard by the captain and his crew. One of them is me. One of them is you. One of them is doing the throwing, the other is being thrown. I'm not sure who is who, you or I. There is no fear, nor shame in this piece of information. There is only the fact of the *Zong* and its unending voyage and those deaths that cannot be undone. Where death has begun but remains unfinished because it recurs. (229–30)

The past surfaces again and again in the present: past injustices keep repeating themselves in present relations.

In an interview, D'Aguiar makes the link between slavery and present-day racism even more explicit. He speaks of there being "a double narrative" in *Feeding the Ghosts*, with "the narrative of [his] own experience" forcing him to find "a precedent from history" which could "sustain [him] in the racist present" (qtd. in Frias 420).

When asked, "To what extent has slavery personally dehumanized you," he offers the following answer, which also touches on his motivations for writing about slavery:

> My black ancestry and Caribbean experience aligns me with a history of slavery. My skin has drawn a lot of static from whites who hate blacks, both in my teenage years growing up in London and since my arrival in the U.S. in 1992 to teach. Stories from the past about the auction block are automatically my stories. I feel on behalf of those who suffered these things. Racism is not over by any means. There are examples of it every day in the media. People die every day at the hands of racists. I deplore these things. I feel them. I write about race to keep the idea of one race as superior to another strange and unacceptable.
>
> (qtd. in Frias 424)

D'Aguiar expresses similar sentiments in "The Last Essay about Slavery," whose publication predates that of *Feeding the Ghosts* by one year. In the essay, he rejects calls "for slavery to be confined to the past once and for all" on the grounds that slavery has a "direct bearing on how the races fail to get along today" (125). Though he would only be too happy to see slavery finally laid to rest, the present unfortunately "refuses to allow slavery to go away" (126). In order to understand and solve present-day conflicts between the races, D'Aguiar argues, it is necessary to examine the slave past (135–36). In his view, the point of engaging in an imaginative act of looking back by writing "another slave novel" (139) is to affect readers' "view of themselves and of the multi-racial world they inhabit"; to get them to redraw "their coveted maps of empathy" by activating "their ability to experience fellow-feeling for someone of a different race, the opposite gender and the power-brokered relationships between and within such groupings" (139). Speaking to the reader "about now as much as about then" (143), contemporary slave novels such as his own "belie any notion of the past being past. In fact they prove, through character, the presence of the past and perhaps even the past in the future. Mexico's premier poet, Octavio Paz, said, 'our greatest enemy is history.' In this instance history is our greatest ally in shaping the future" (144).

At the heart of D'Aguiar's testimonial enterprise, then—and this is also true, it seems to me, for Dabydeen—there is a concern with justice, not only for the dead, but also for the living and the as yet unborn. Their works conjure the ghosts of victims of racial violence without, ultimately, conjuring them away in the name of a supposedly redeemed present, free from the burdens of the past. Rather than affirm a clear distinction between the past and the present, they demonstrate how those two are imbricated in one another, as the past continues to structure the present. Thus, they unsettle triumphalist accounts of the postcolonial that deny the continuing effects of racial and colonial trauma. Dabydeen and D'Aguiar's relationship to history should be construed, then, not as a pathological attachment but as an assumption of ethico-political responsibility. Sam Durrant's description of the work of postcolonial mourning as performed by J. M. Coetzee, Toni Morrison, and Wilson Harris applies to Dabydeen and D'Aguiar just as well: "they bear witness to the various histories of racial oppression that underwrite local, national, and international privilege and continue to inform, if not determine, our cultural and psychological existence in the hope that their literary witnessing will bring into being a truly *post*colonial form of community" (2). By opening their art to "the fully realized presence of a haunting," they practise "a postcolonial ethics—and aesthetics—of hospitality" (Durrant 14). Moreover, their extension of hospitality to ghosts invites a similar response from the reader, who is given an opportunity to learn to live with ghosts and thereby, perhaps, to become a scholar of the future.

6
Cross-Traumatic Affiliation

If, as Cathy Caruth observes in *Unclaimed Experience*, "history, like trauma, is never simply one's own, ... history is precisely the way we are implicated in each other's traumas" (24), then traumatic colonial histories not only have to be acknowledged more fully, on their own terms, and in their own terms, but they also have to be considered in relation to traumatic metropolitan or First World histories for trauma studies to have any hope of redeeming its promise of ethical effectiveness. In Chapter 1, we already briefly touched upon the problems involved in (interpreting) encounters between different individual or collective traumas in relation to Caruth's analysis of *Hiroshima mon amour*, and Chapter 4 explored the bonds of sorrow that unite a privileged white American mother and a poor black South African one in Sindiwe Magona's novel *Mother to Mother*. The current chapter investigates the inherent relationality of history and trauma by tracing memorial connections between the Holocaust—the historical calamity that has attracted by far the most attention from the Euro-American academy—and histories of colonial suffering as forged in various theoretical writings. As Karyn Ball has argued in relation to the United States context, "If trauma studies might be said to have a political and ethical task, it would be to continue to move beyond the iconic logic of the 'unprecedented' [associated with the Holocaust] and to employ the strategy of comparison in order to forge links among traumatic histories that would raise Americans' historical consciousness and promote their sense of civic responsibility" (15). I will discuss attempts to theorize the co-implication of Holocaust and colonial trauma against the background

72

of, firstly, the recent broadening of the focus of the field of memory studies—of which trauma theory is a subfield—from the national to the transnational level, and, secondly, efforts to bridge a disciplinary divide between Jewish and postcolonial studies preventing the Holocaust and histories of slavery and colonial domination from being considered in a common frame. The next two chapters examine how literature reflects and elicits a relational understanding of trauma by analysing a number of literary texts in which the legacies of the Holocaust and colonialism come into contact.

Memory beyond the nation-state

As is well known, memory emerged as an urgent topic of debate in the humanities in the 1980s. The last few decades have seen a profusion of important work on memory, leading some to speak of a "memory boom" (Winter). A great deal of research has been devoted to "collective memory," a term developed by Maurice Halbwachs in the 1920s to denote collectively shared representations of the past (*On Collective Memory*, 1992), or "cultural memory," a related concept coined by Jan Assmann in the 1980s which stresses the role of institutionalized canons of culture in the formation and transmission of collective memories (*Das kulturelle Gedächtnis: Schrift, Erinnerung, und Identität in den frühen Hochkulturen*, 1992). Early work in memory studies focused on the ways in which memories are shared within particular communities and constitute or reinforce group identity. Very often, most notably in Pierre Nora's monumental *Lieux de mémoire* (*Realms of Memory*, 1996–1998 [1984–1992]) project, the nation-state has been taken as paradigmatic of such mnemonic communities. As Aleida Assmann and Sebastian Conrad point out, "Until recently, the dynamics of memory production unfolded primarily within the bounds of the nation state; coming to terms with the past was largely a national project" (2).

In the last few years, however, the transnational and even global dissemination of memory has moved to the centre of attention. As Daniel Levy and Natan Sznaider put it, the "container of the nation-state" in which the conventional concept of collective memory is embedded "is in the process of slowly being cracked" (2). The emphasis in memory studies is gradually shifting from static sites of memory to the dynamic movement of memory. Several factors account for this development. Assmann and Conrad note that memories travel across national borders through a range of different channels, including human carriers, transnational institutions and networks, and the mass media. In part, the increased mobility of memory is a consequence of pervasive migration flows. Memories migrate from one country to another, and from one continent to another, with individuals: "As migrants carry their heritage, memories and traumas with them, these are transferred and brought into new social constellations and political contexts" (A. Assmann and Conrad 2). Memories are also increasingly transmitted and supported via transnational institutions and networks, such as the European Union, the United Nations, UNESCO, and non-governmental organizations. However, the most important factor in the transnational and global dissemination of memories are the mass media, including television, film, and the Internet. Thanks to the rise of mass cultural technologies, memories themselves have become more mobile, more transportable. With the aid of these technologies, it has become increasingly possible for people to take on memories of events not "their own," events that they did not live through themselves and to which they have no familial, ethnic, or national tie—a phenomenon which Alison Landsberg has usefully labelled "prosthetic memory."

Arguments about the transnationalization or globalization of memory typically reference the Holocaust, still the primary, archetypal topic in memory studies. In the second half of the 1990s, for example, Alvin Rosenfeld, Hilene Flanzbaum, and Peter Novick called attention to the so-called Americanization of the Holocaust. While reaching back at least as far as the theatrical and cinematic versions of the Anne Frank story in the 1950s, this process of Americanization began in earnest with the enormous success of the 1978 television mini-series *Holocaust*, a media event that influenced popular reception and memory of the Nazi genocide across national and identitarian boundaries.[1] The transnational resonance of the Holocaust did not stop there, though. In *The Holocaust and Memory in the Global Age* (2006 [2001]), Levy and Sznaider argue that the global spread of Holocaust discourse has generated a new form of memory, "cosmopolitan memory," which they define as "a memory that harbors the possibility of transcending ethnic and national boundaries" (4).[2] In their view, the Holocaust has escaped its spatial and temporal particularism to emerge as a common moral touchstone in the wake of the Cold War, "an age of uncertainty" marked by "the absence of master ideological narratives" (18). The negative memory of the extermination of the Jews can serve as a universal moral norm, they argue, and thus help foster a human-rights culture and advance the cause of global justice. Nowadays, victims of human-rights violations who seek recognition for their suffering often analogize their experience to that of the Jews during the Holocaust and compare the perpetrators to the Nazis. The Nazi genocide functions as a global narrative template, which is used to conceptualize and to demand recognition for marginalized or ignored acts of injustice and traumatic histories across the globe. The fact that the Holocaust has become "a floating signifier" that easily attaches itself to "historically very different situations" (Huyssen, *Present Pasts* 99) is borne out by terms such as "Kosovocaust," "African Holocaust," "American Holocaust," "nuclear Holocaust," and "abortion Holocaust."

If Levy and Sznaider are to be believed, this is an inherently positive development, because it supposedly leads to a worldwide increase in democracy, tolerance, and human rights. In support of this view, they point to the fact that the global diffusion of the memory of the Holocaust has legitimized international interventions in the conduct of nations that are committing atrocities, interventions that were unthinkable until recently. International courts now pass judgement on political and military leaders who have been indicted for crimes against humanity. The best example of this is the military intervention by NATO in Kosovo in 1999 to halt the genocide against the Kosovo Albanians that was being carried out by the Yugoslav army. The NATO campaign was legitimized through the slogan "Never again Auschwitz" and led to the main culprit, the Yugoslav president Slobodan Milosevic, being brought to justice in The Hague (Levy and Sznaider 18).

In an essay titled "The Social Construction of Moral Universals," originally published in 2002, Jeffrey Alexander puts forward an argument similar to Levy and Sznaider's.[3] Over the last 50 years, he contends, the Holocaust, a specific historical event that was extremely traumatic for "a delimited particular group," has been transformed into "a generalized symbol of human suffering and moral evil" and redefined as "a traumatic event for all of humankind" (3). Through symbolic extension and emotional identification, Alexander maintains, the Holocaust has become a universal "sacred-evil" myth that holds out "historically unprecedented opportunities for ethnic, racial, and religious justice, for mutual recognition, and for global conflicts becoming regulated in a more civil way" (3). The diffusion of the Holocaust metaphor has "deepened contemporary sensitivity to social evil," made us aware that "evil is inside all of us and in every society," and enlarged the human imagination to such an extent that, for the first time in history, it is capable of "identifying, understanding, and judging the kinds of genocidal mass killings in which national, ethnic, and ideological groupings continue to engage today" (35).

In the past decade, Levy and Sznaider's book and Alexander's essay, both landmarks in the fledgling field of what Astrid Erll calls "transcultural memory studies," have been criticized for a number of reasons.[4] Among other things, they have been accused of being naively optimistic about the consequences of the global dissemination of Holocaust memory. Levy and Sznaider as well as Alexander largely ignore the fact that, as I will presently show, the Holocaust is often used in ways that do not lead to greater transcultural understanding and the establishment of a universal human-rights culture. The fact that both texts were written in the pre-9/11 era may partly explain this. After all, visions of a cosmopolitan future seemed more plausible then than they have done ever since the 9/11 terrorist attacks, as the so-called war on terror that was declared in their wake seemed to make real the "clash of civilizations" between "Islam" and "the West" posited by Samuel Huntington. In fact, in retrospective accounts of their earlier work, both Levy and Sznaider and Alexander have acknowledged that it was the product of a more innocent time. In a postscript to *Remembering the Holocaust: A Debate* (2009) in which he responds to his critics (albeit, curiously, only in the footnotes), Alexander reminds the reader that he researched and composed his essay in "the late 1990s," which, "[i]n retrospect," can be seen as a time of "cautious optimism".

> The American and European intervention in Kosovo had just given strong evidence for the universalizing power of the Holocaust effect. Dictatorships were still being turned into democracies, and there was a bubbling effervescence about the emergence of global civil society. It was a time to focus on the emergence of global narratives about the possibility of justice, among

which there is no more surprising and inspiring story than the transvaluation of the Holocaust.

("On the Global and Local Representations
of the Holocaust Tragedy" 177)

Now, however, we live in "a darker time, more divided, more violent, more tense. We have become less optimistic about the creation of a global civil society, more sensitive to the continuing festering of local wounds" ("On the Global and Local Representations of the Holocaust Tragedy" 177). Likewise, in the revised introduction to the 2006 English edition of their book, which came out five years after the original German version, Levy and Sznaider express their awareness that times have changed: "This book was conceived in 1999, long before the so-called midlife crisis of the human-rights regime and before the first epochal event of the twenty-first century—namely, the terrorist attacks of September 11, 2001" (19).

As many commentators have noted, Levy and Sznaider and Alexander tend to ignore or minimize the fact that the memory of the Holocaust is often mobilized for immoral purposes. A. Dirk Moses, for example, argues that the Holocaust is typically invoked not with the cosmopolitan effect that Levy and Sznaider suppose but "to express the fear of collective destruction: the apocalypse of genocide," a usage which "contributes towards terroristic political action in the form of pre-emptive strikes and anticipatory self-defence to forestall feared destruction" ("Genocide and the Terror of History" 91). Israel, the society where the Holocaust is at the very centre of collective memory, is frequently mentioned in this context as a case in point.[5] Israel has repeatedly used the memory of the Holocaust to legitimize extreme violence against the Palestinians and neighbouring Arab countries. Visions of a "second Holocaust" allegedly facing the Jewish people from the Palestinians resisting the occupation or from Arab states in the region have often been used by Zionists as part of a strategy to justify whatever Israel does as self-defence. As Robert Manne argues, for the majority of Israeli Jews the lesson of the Holocaust is not universalist but resolutely particularist: not "It will never happen again" but, rather, "It will never happen to us again" (142). In this case, Holocaust rhetoric operates "more as a metaphorical fortress than as a bridge" (Manne 145). Another example of a situation in which the Holocaust metaphor provided not an increase in justice but contributed to a catastrophic loss of life is the Iraq War. George W. Bush repeatedly used Nazi comparisons to rally support for his illegal pre-emptive war against Iraq in 2003, waged in the name of human rights, which resulted in the overthrow of Saddam Hussein and the violent deaths of thousands of people.[6] Bush compared Saddam to Hitler, and suggested that his gas attacks on the Kurds and Iranians during the Iran-Iraq war amounted to a holocaust. With Manne, then, we can conclude that "[w]hen the sacred-evil myth of the Holocaust becomes entangled in politics, it often becomes depressingly profane" (145).

While it is undeniable that references to the Holocaust are increasingly being used to call attention to and demand recognition for other traumas, atrocities, and injustices, to claim that Holocaust memory has become a harbinger of a universal human-rights culture is to overlook vast amounts of evidence of Holocaust comparisons serving dubious and questionable purposes. The comparative argument can be exploited for revisionist ends and serve to relativize, dilute, or erase the memory of the Holocaust by homogenizing very different histories. A good example of this phenomenon can be found in the *Historikerstreit* or Historians' Debate of the mid-1980s, a controversy over the interpretation of the Holocaust between left-wing and right-wing intellectuals in West Germany. A number of conservative historians, led by Ernst Nolte, compared the Holocaust to the Soviet terror under Joseph Stalin and to Germany's own losses (the mass expulsions of ethnic Germans from Czechoslovakia and Poland at the end of the Second World War) in order to diminish the importance of the Holocaust and to dilute the singularity of German responsibility for it. Progressive intellectuals, most prominently the philosopher Jürgen Habermas, insisted on the uniqueness of the Holocaust as a defence against this relativistic position, which sought to minimize Nazi crimes. To give another example, in his book *The Fire. The Bombing of Germany, 1940–1945* (2006 [2002]) the German author and historian Jörg Friedrich attempts to deflect German guilt for the Holocaust by claiming moral equivalency between the Allied firebombing of Dresden and the Nazi extermination of the Jews. To reinforce his claims, he uses terms from the Nazi vocabulary of the Holocaust to characterize the roles and actions of the Allied bombing crews: he describes the cellars of the houses as "gas chambers" and the pilots of the air raids as "SS Einsatzgruppen."

As Andreas Huyssen (*Present Pasts*) and Miriam Hansen have pointed out, Holocaust comparisons can also work as "screen memories"—meaning that the Holocaust is remembered in order to repress other instances of historical oppression which are more immediate and closer to home—or simply hinder understanding of specific local histories. "Screen memory" is a term coined by Freud to designate a memory that hides another, more distressing memory ("Screen Memories"). It can be argued that, especially in the United States, but also in various European countries, the Holocaust is remembered in order to displace, repress, or "screen" awkward episodes from one's own national past: the genocide of the Native Americans, slavery and segregation, nuclear warfare, and the Vietnam War in the case of the United States; colonial history and collaboration with the Nazis in the case of Europe. The enormous amount of attention paid to the Holocaust and the extraordinary importance attached to this event, so the argument goes, serve to blind Americans and Europeans to certain unpalatable aspects of their own history.[7] However, Levy and Sznaider and Alexander misread the impact of the globalization of Holocaust memory and underestimate the negative, harmful uses to which Holocaust comparisons can be and have been put.

Another important criticism that has been levelled both at Levy and Sznaider and at Alexander is that their analysis is marred by Eurocentrism. For one thing, their work tends to conflate the West—to which their research is actually limited—with the world. Levy and Sznaider only look at the cases of Germany, the United States, and Israel, extrapolating their conclusions from this narrow and anything but random sample to the entire world. Alexander, for his part, despite his bold title, emphasizes that he is talking about "the West," by which, it seems, he means Europe and the United States. As Martin Jay points out, "although his argument about universalization begins by claiming that it [the Holocaust] has reached global proportions, he ends by conceding that it has made only modest inroads in non-Western cultures that were far away from the actual events" (106). Indeed, in a short section at the very end of his essay titled "Is the Holocaust Western?" Alexander acknowledges that there are many parts of the world—including Latin America and "Hindu, Buddhist, Confucian, Islamic, African, and still-communist regions and regimes" (69)—where the Holocaust is not a common reference.

These non-Western regions and nations tend to be preoccupied with historical traumas that they themselves suffered, in many cases those of Western imperialism.[8] Alexander has his doubts as to whether people in these other parts of the world can attain the same level of moral maturity as Westerners: "Can countries or civilizations that do not acknowledge the Holocaust develop universalistic political moralities?" (69). While he leaves the question unanswered, the fact that he asks it in the first place is telling. As Aleida Assmann has remarked, "Alexander here affirms the uniqueness and sacredness of the Holocaust as a touchstone of universal moral maturity. Nations that do not embrace the Holocaust are proving that they cannot reach this higher level" (108). Indeed, Alexander appears to use the Holocaust as "a yardstick for moral ranking" (108).

In fact, both Levy and Sznaider's and Alexander's studies display what Avishai Margalit has called "the danger of biased salience" accompanying the construction of a shared moral memory for mankind: because they are generally better remembered, the atrocities of Europe are perceived as morally more significant than atrocities elsewhere (80). Their work is symptomatic of a wider tendency among Western scholars to regard "the genocide of European peoples in the twentieth century" as "a more urgent research question than the genocide of non-Europeans by Europeans in the preceding centuries or by postcolonial states of their indigenous populations today" (Moses, "Conceptual Blockages" 9). As Moses has argued, this asymmetry rests on the assumption that the Holocaust is unique, unprecedented, and singular, which implies that colonial and indigenous genocides are lesser, incomplete, marginal, or even primitive genocides (if they are considered genocides at all), and thus reinforces Eurocentrism ("Conceptual Blockages" 9). Instead of promoting transcultural solidarity, Levy and Sznaider's and Alexander's claims about the universality of the Holocaust, which they see as a unique source of universal moral lessons that presumably cannot be learnt from any other event, can be interpreted as "a form of Euro-American imperialism in the field of memory" (A. Assmann and Conrad 9).

Bridging the gap between Jewish and postcolonial studies

If the traditional national focus of memory studies is one explanation for why there has so far been relatively little research on the interrelatedness of memories of the Holocaust and colonial suffering, another is the gaping disciplinary divide that has long separated Jewish and postcolonial studies, despite a host of shared concerns. Bryan Cheyette, Sam Durrant, Paul Gilroy, and Michael Rothberg have remarked on the conspicuous lack of interaction between the two fields, both of which grapple with the legacies of histories of violence perpetrated in the name of racist ideologies and imperialist political projects. In the introduction to a recent special issue of *Wasafiri* devoted to "Jewish/Postcolonial Diasporas," Cheyette notes that histories of victimization such as the Holocaust and colonial oppression, and the literatures dealing with these respective histories, are being thought of in isolation as a result of "the narrowness and exclusions of the academy" (2). Histories and literatures are limited to "separate spheres" by "our professional guilds," as "[n]ew disciplinary formations—postcolonial studies, diaspora studies, ethnic studies, Jewish studies and Holocaust studies—tend to define themselves in relation to what they exclude" (2). In his book *Between Camps: Nations, Cultures and the Allure of Race* (2004 [2000]), which extends the argument first made in the last chapter of *The Black Atlantic: Modernity and Double Consciousness* (1993) about the need to make connections across black and Jewish diasporic histories, Gilroy asks: "Why does it remain so difficult for so many people to accept the knotted intersection of histories produced by this fusion of horizons?" (78).

Cheyette addresses just this question in an earlier article, in which he explores theoretical impediments that prevent postcolonial studies from incorporating Jewish history into a broader understanding of a colonizing Western modernity ("Venetian Spaces" 53). Continuities and overlaps between Jewish and colonial experience have remained underexplored, Cheyette points out, because of the reluctance or inability of many postcolonial theorists to perceive Jews as anything other than as part of a supposedly homogeneous white, "Judeo-Christian" majoritarian tradition ("Venetian Spaces" 54). Such a stance "flattens out the ambivalent position of Jews," who, while historically at the heart of European metropolitan culture, were at the same time banished from its privileged sphere ("Venetian Spaces" 55). By talking about a dominant Western "Judeo-Christian" tradition, postcolonial theory denies Jews minority status and dismisses them as simple beneficiaries if not enablers or perpetrators of European oppression.

Cheyette gives three reasons to explain postcolonial theory's resistance to breaking down the separate spheres between Jews and other ethnicities. The first of these is the past complicity of many individual Jews with the colonial enterprise. The most famous example of this phenomenon is the Jewish-born British prime minister Benjamin Disraeli, who "successfully promoted English Jingoism along with the Victorian cult of Empire" ("Venetian Spaces" 55). One may also think here of Christopher Columbus, the man who started the European colonization of the Americas: according to some scholars, Columbus was a Sephardic Jew who tried to conceal his Jewish heritage (Irizarry; Wiesenthal). Secondly, there is the history of Zionism, which points to Jewish collusion with colonial practices that continues to this day. Israel's occupation of the Palestinian territories is widely seen as a form of settler colonialism, which partly explains why postcolonial critics have tended to be less than eager to recognize Jews as victims of imperialism. After all, as Ivan Davidson Kalmar and Derek Penslar observe in the introduction to their edited collection *Orientalism and the Jews* (2005),

> Focusing on Jews as targets rather than perpetrators of orientalism ... decreases (in rhetorical terms though certainly not in logical ones) the effectiveness of the argument that Zionism is a form of anti-Arab orientalism. It is, therefore, perhaps understandable if writers primarily concerned with a critique of Zionism overlook other aspects of the relationship between orientalism and the Jews. They generally see Zionism as an example of orientalist ideology in the service of western colonialism, and consequently link the creation of Israel to the West's imperial expansion in the Orient. (xv)

While "the link between Zionism and colonialism is undeniable," Kalmar and Penslar continue, "there is more to Zionism than that: it has also been a response to racist discrimination, and the discrimination has often been expressed in orientalist terms" (xv). Indeed, in many respects, Zionism is itself "an anticolonial liberation movement" (xxxvi). Thirdly, Cheyette points to tensions in contemporary black-Jewish relations in the United States, both within and outside the academy, which have reinforced the compartmentalization of black and Jewish histories and literatures. At the heart of the problem is the perceived appropriation of black experience by the Jewish community. The Holocaust has achieved mainstream recognition in the United States, making it, as noted above, "a convenient filter through which other more immediate American histories of oppression—such as the history of slavery and the genocide of Native Americans—can be under-played" (Cheyette, "Venetian Spaces" 58). The Americanization of the Holocaust, Cheyette goes on, "allows the United States to forget or play down its policies of genocide and racial oppression on its own back door," which explains why black-Jewish relations in the United States have become increasingly strained since the late 1960s ("Venetian Spaces" 58).

While Cheyette's focus is on the diffidence shown by postcolonial studies towards Jewish studies, it is fair to say that the feeling is mutual. Indeed, further complicating the dialogue between Jewish and postcolonial studies is a strongly-held belief in the uniqueness of the Holocaust among many Jewish studies scholars. As Rothberg points out, the proponents of uniqueness typically refuse to consider the Holocaust and other catastrophic histories in a common frame: they "assiduously search out and refute all attempts to compare or analogize the Holocaust in order to preserve memory of the Shoah from its dilution or relativization" (*Multidirectional Memory* 9). As we have seen in the cases of Alexander and Levy and Sznaider, though, uniqueness thinking can paradoxically go hand in hand with a belief in comparability—as Alexander points out in a section of his essay titled "The Dilemma of Uniqueness," it was the very fact that the Holocaust came to be regarded as a unique event that "compelled it to become generalized and departicularized" (58).[9] Critics of uniqueness or of the politics of Holocaust memory, on the other hand, "often argue ... that the ever-increasing interest in the Nazi genocide distracts from the consideration of other historical tragedies" (Rothberg, *Multidirectional Memory* 9)—this is, of course, the third reason adduced by Cheyette to explain postcolonial theory's cold-shouldering of Jewish history. In fact, a common critical response to the privileging of the Holocaust is to claim uniqueness or primacy for other histories of suffering, such as African American slavery or the genocide of the Native Americans. While such efforts have helped raise the profile of these relatively neglected histories, they are historically problematic as well as politically and ethically unproductive. Insisting on the distinctiveness and difference of one's own history can indicate a kind of blindness, a refusal to recognize the larger historical processes of which that history is a part. Moreover, claims for the uniqueness of the suffering of the particular victim group to which one belongs tend to deny the capacity for, or the effectiveness of, transcultural empathy.

Though, generally speaking, there has been little interaction between Jewish and postcolonial studies, a number of theorists and historians have long recognized continuities between the history of the European Jews and the history of European colonialism. In the early 1950s Hannah Arendt put forward the so-called boomerang thesis, according to which European totalitarianism, and Nazism in particular, has its roots in overseas colonialism. She identified an inextricable interrelationship between the phenomena of anti-Semitism, imperialism, and totalitarianism, which, in the preface to *The Origins of Totalitarianism* (2004 [1951]), she named "[t]he subterranean stream of Western history" (xxvii).[10] Around the same time Aimé Césaire argued, in *Discourse on Colonialism* (2000 [1950]), that Nazism should be viewed as the continuation of Europe's treatment of various non-European peoples in the previous centuries. Hitler, he suggested, "applied to Europe colonialist procedures which until then had been reserved exclusively for the Arabs of Algeria, the coolies of India, and the blacks of Africa" (14). A few years earlier W. E. B. Du Bois had already claimed, in *The World and Africa: An Inquiry into the Part Which Africa Has Played in World History* (1947), that "[t]here was no Nazi atrocity—concentration camps, wholesale maiming and murder, defilement of women or ghastly blasphemy of childhood—which the Christian civilization of Europe had not long been practicing against colored folk in all parts of the world in the name of and for the defense of a Superior Race born to rule the world" (23).[11] This understanding of Nazism as colonialism revisited on Europe also informs more recent research in the fledgling field of comparative genocide studies by scholars such as Mark Mazower, A. Dirk Moses, David Moshman, Jacques Semelin, Timothy Snyder, Dan Stone, and Jürgen Zimmerer, who have all sought to remove the "conceptual blockages" (Moses) in comparing modern atrocities, to move beyond notions of the Holocaust's uniqueness that might inscribe a hierarchy of suffering across modernity, and to elicit the structural continuities and discontinuities between atrocious events.

There has so far been little parallel work by literary and cultural critics; notable exceptions include Michael Rothberg, Bryan Cheyette, Sam Durrant, Max Silverman, Paul Gilroy, Robert Eaglestone, and Aamir Mufti. A particularly noteworthy intervention is Rothberg's monograph *Multidirectional Memory: Remembering the Holocaust in the Age of Decolonization* (2009), which illuminates what he calls the "multidirectional" orientation of collective memory. Rothberg offers an alternative to the "competitive memory" model—shared, as he points out, by many proponents and critics of uniqueness—according to which the capacity to remember historical tragedies is limited and any attention to one tragedy inevitably diminishes our capacity to remember another. Against this framework, which understands collective memory as "a zero-sum struggle over scarce resources," he suggests that we consider memory as multidirectional, that is, "as subject to ongoing negotiation, cross-referencing, and borrowing; as productive and not privative" (3). The concept of multidirectional memory "draw[s] attention to the dynamic transfers that take place between diverse places and times during the act of remembrance" (11). In a recent special issue of *Yale French Studies* on multidirectional memory in French and Francophone culture that he guest-edited together with Debarati Sanyal and Max Silverman, Rothberg coins the term *nœuds de mémoire* ("knots of memory") to denote points of contact between the memories and legacies of the Holocaust, colonialism, and slavery. The term obviously plays on Nora's *lieux de mémoire* ("sites of memory"), suggesting that Nora's static model has reached its limits and that we need a new, dynamic model of remembrance. Rothberg considers memory to be inherently comparative, but he disputes the idea that comparisons between atrocities inevitably erase the differences between them and imply a false equivalence. In focusing on the Holocaust, he seeks to avoid the twin pitfalls of sacralization and trivialization: the tendency, on the one hand, to emphasize the distinctness of the Holocaust to such an extent that it cannot be compared to anything else; and, on the other, to relativize or dilute its memory by homogenizing very different histories.

Rothberg's specific concern is with the mutually enabling relationship between Holocaust memory and memories of the struggle for decolonization. As we have seen, Levy and Sznaider and Alexander assume that the Holocaust is central in that it allows other histories of victimization to be articulated. According to Rothberg, however, the process is not that simple. Multidirectional memory is not "a one-way street" (*Multidirectional Memory* 6): just as the Holocaust has enabled the articulation of other histories, so these other histories have helped shape the way we think about the Holocaust and affected the way Holocaust memory has circulated. In other words, the process is dialogical or multidirectional, not monological or unidirectional. In fact, in a critical response to Alexander's essay in *Remembering the Holocaust*, Rothberg suggests "the need to disarticulate notions of universalism from Americanization and bring to view the heterogeneity of exchanges between memory of the Holocaust and memory of other histories of trauma and extreme violence" ("Multidirectional Memory" 125). He challenges Alexander's almost exclusive focus on the United States and emphasizes the dialogical nature of the process by which moral universals are constructed, which "entails the redefinition of both what the Holocaust means and what the events to which it is imaginatively attached mean" ("Multidirectional Memory" 129). The Holocaust, for Rothberg, does not become "a floating, universal signifier" but "emerges in its specificity as part of a multidirectional network of diverse histories of extreme violence, torture, and racist policy" ("Multidirectional Memory" 132). The example that clinches this argument in his book is that of Holocaust memory in France. Rothberg shows that the Algerian War of Independence (1954–1962) helped bring about the conditions in which the Holocaust could be publicly remembered. At the time, many intellectuals pointed out that the colonial violence of the French state in Algeria, and particularly the use of torture and detention camps, echoed the methods of the Nazis. Rothberg contends that, along with the Eichmann trial, the protest against contemporary events in Algeria and in Paris helped enable the emergence of public Holocaust memory in France in the early 1960s.

Besides making a theoretical argument against a logic of competitive memory based on the zero-sum game and a historical argument about the inseparability of memories of the Holocaust and colonial violence, Rothberg also puts forward a political argument in *Multidirectional Memory*. He questions the taken-for-granted link between collective memory and group identity—the assumption that a straight line connects, for example, Jewish memory and Jewish identity or African American memory and African American identity in mutual confirmation. Rothberg rejects the idea that the only kinds of memories and identities that are possible are "ones that exclude elements of alterity and forms of commonality with others" (4–5). Memories do not have exclusive owners; they do not naturally belong to any particular group. Rather, the borders of memory and identity are "jagged" (5). Going beyond the common sense of identity politics, Rothberg suggests that the productive, intercultural dynamic of multidirectional memory has the potential to create "new forms of solidarity and new visions of justice" (5). However, he also recognizes that multidirectional memory can function "in the interest of violence or exclusion instead of solidarity" (12). This is often the case, for example, with the invocation of the Holocaust in the context of the Israeli-Palestinian conflict—briefly discussed in the epilogue of his book—which tends to take the form of "a ritual trading of threats and insults" (311). Rothberg returns to the Israeli-Palestinian situation in an article included in a recent special issue of *Criticism* on the topic of transcultural negotiations of Holocaust memory that he and I co-edited, where he engages with "some of the more difficult and even troubling cases of multidirectionality" ("From Gaza to Warsaw" 524). Even though public memory is structurally multidirectional, he argues, in the sense of always being marked by "transcultural borrowing, exchange, and adaptation," the politics of multidirectional memory does not therefore "come[] with any guarantees" ("From Gaza to Warsaw" 524). Rothberg sets out to develop "an ethics of comparison that can distinguish politically productive forms of memory from those that lead to competition, appropriation, or trivialization" ("From Gaza to Warsaw" 525). He attempts to map the different forms that public memory can take in politically charged situations: "By mapping that discursive field, I arrive at a four-part distinction in which multidirectional memories are located at the intersection of an *axis of comparison* (defined by a continuum stretching from equation to differentiation) and an *axis of political affect* (defined by a continuum stretching from solidarity to competition—two complex, composite affects)" ("From Gaza to Warsaw" 525). Memory discourses that combine differentiation and solidarity offer "a greater political potential," he maintains, than those that rely on equation and competition ("From Gaza to Warsaw" 526). He concludes that "a radically democratic politics of memory needs to include a differentiated empirical history, moral solidarity with victims of diverse injustices, and an ethics of comparison that coordinates the asymmetrical claims of those victims" ("From Gaza to Warsaw" 526).

In *Multidirectional Memory*, Rothberg engages with an important but largely overlooked archive of literary as well as theoretical and cinematic texts that bring histories of genocide, slavery, and colonialism together and let them address one another. The next two chapters seek to expand and contribute to the study of this archive by examining how, why, and to what effect the work of Caryl Phillips, which Rothberg also discusses, and Anita Desai's novel *Baumgartner's Bombay*, which he does not, relate traumas associated with the Holocaust and (post)colonial suffering to one another.[12] I will explore the nature of the imaginative connections that the texts establish between these different histories, the meaning of the new perspectives on the past that are opened up, and the ethico-political stakes involved in the reconfiguration of culturally prevalent concepts and frameworks of memory.

7
Jewish/Postcolonial Diasporas in the Work of Caryl Phillips

In this chapter, I will investigate the links forged between memories of black and Jewish suffering in the fiction and non-fiction of the British Caribbean writer Caryl Phillips, one master of the genre Rebecca Walkowitz has called "comparison literature."[1] In his novels *Higher Ground* (1989) and *The Nature of Blood* (1997), as well as in his travel book *The European Tribe* (1987), Phillips interweaves stories of anti-Semitic and racist violence set in many different times and places.[2] After illuminating the connections between the different histories established in these texts through the rhetorical tropes of metaphor and metonymy, understood not only as poetic devices but also in the extended sense of deep structures of thought that determine the way one looks at history (White), I will argue that Phillips's work seeks to foster attunement to multiple histories of suffering and to move beyond various tribalisms by supplementing a metaphorical view of history, which, in its insistence on similarity, theatens to conflate distinct historical experiences, with a metonymical view, which places them alongside one another and thus preserves the distance between them. Dismantling anti-comparativist impulses, Phillips's work can be seen to present a fuller picture of the dark underside of modernity and to pave the way for alliances and solidarities that transcend race, ethnicity, nationality, religion, and culture.

Caryl Phillips and the Jewish experience

Phillips's interest in Jewishness is not due to any family connections, though he is in fact partly Jewish. As he reveals in his collection of

essays and reviews *A New World Order* (2001), his maternal grandfather, Emmanuel de Fraites, was "a Jewish trader with Portuguese
roots that reached back to the island of Madeira" ("The Gift of Displacement" 130). However, Phillips did not learn about this Jewish
ancestor until the 1980s; his fascination with the Holocaust started
much earlier. In his essay "In the Ghetto," included in *The European
Tribe*, he notes that his interest in the Nazi genocide can be traced
back to his experience of growing up black in Britain at a time when
there was little informed public discussion of his own situation: "As a
child, in what seemed to me a hostile country, the Jews were the
only minority group discussed with reference to exploitation and
racialism, and for that reason, I naturally identified with them" (54).
Having no access to any representations of slavery, colonialism, or
their legacies, Phillips tried to make sense of his experience and history through the prism of Jewish suffering: "The bloody excesses of
colonialism, the pillage and rape of modern Africa, the transporta-
tion of 11 million black people to the Americas, and their subsequent
bondage were not on the curriculum, and certainly not on the television screen. As a result I vicariously channelled a part of my hurt
and frustration through the Jewish experience" (54). Phillips's earliest response to the Holocaust, then, was one of substitution: there
being no public reference points for the black experience in Britain,
the Holocaust was made to fill that void.[3]

The metaphorical logic underlying Phillips's relationship to Jewish
history at this point in his youth also informs his earliest literary production. As he reveals elsewhere in *The European Tribe*, in an essay
titled "Anne Frank's Amsterdam," the first piece of fiction he ever
wrote, as a teenager, was "[a] short story about a fifteen-year-old
Jewish boy in Amsterdam" (67) who manages to escape transporta-
tion to a concentration camp and is saved by a farmer. He wrote
this story, which obviously has an element of wish-fulfilment about
it, after seeing a programme on television. an episode of the *World
at War* series about the Nazi occupation of Holland and the subsequent rounding up of the Jews had made a deep impression on him,
summoning up feelings of "outrage and fear" (66). Watching library
footage of Bergen-Belsen and Auschwitz, he realized not only "the
enormity of the crime that was being committed" but also "the precariousness of my own position in Europe" (66). After all, "[i]f white
people could do that to white people, what the hell would they do to

me?" (67). As Phillips has since remarked of the story he went on to write, "The Dutch boy was, of course, me. A fourteen year old black boy...in working-class Yorkshire in the North of England" ("On 'The Nature of Blood'" 6).

It is clear, then, that Phillips has drawn inspiration from Jewish history right from the start of his career as a writer. However, when he later revisits the Holocaust in his "Jewish" novels *Higher Ground* and *The Nature of Blood*, he implicitly criticizes and checks his initial impulse to analogize black with Jewish suffering. As Wendy Zierler points out, *Higher Ground* and *The Nature of Blood* are "an outgrowth of this early impulse," but "instead of presenting his black experience as equal or directly analogous to Jewish experience, Phillips's novels argue for contiguity, not sameness" (58). More precisely, they are marked by a "dialectic of difference and sameness" (58), as Phillips plants within his narratives "thematic seeds of connection and mutual engagement" but "preserves distance and difference by telling discrete stories that take place at different times and places, using markedly different narrative points of view, which he then interweaves to explore the larger themes of exile, memory, and alienation" (58). It should be noted, though, that this metonymical logic is not entirely absent in *The European Tribe* either, as the young writer's identification with Jewishness does not take the form of a "full-scale metaphoric substitution of one identity or history for another" (Rothberg, *Multidirectional Memory* 156). As Rothberg points out, "Phillips's childhood vicarious experience...represents an alternative to notions of competitive memory: the other's history does not screen out one's own past, but rather serves as a screen for multidirectional projections in which solidarity and self-construction merge" (*Multidirectional Memory* 156). In what follows, I will discuss how the metaphorical and metonymical logics at work in the two "Jewish" novels that emerged out of *The European Tribe* operate.

Parallel histories in *Higher Ground* and *The Nature of Blood*

Both *Higher Ground* and *The Nature of Blood* are obvious examples of what Walkowitz calls "the anthological novel" ("Comparison Literature" 571), by which she means novels that borrow the structure and strategies of the anthology, sampling and collating stories of—in

Phillips's case—racism and anti-Semitism. The anthology is a useful model for Phillips in that "it articulates at the level of form the
problems of order, inclusion, and comparison that migration narratives articulate at the level of content" (Walkowitz, "Location" 537).
Aptly described on the book's dust-jacket as "a haunting triptych of
the dispossessed and the abandoned—of those whose very humanity is being stripped away," *Higher Ground* features the story of an
unnamed African who works as an agent and interpreter in a British
slave-trading fort on the west coast of Africa in the late eighteenth
century ("Heartland"); the story of Rudy Williams, a young black
American detained in a high-security prison for armed robbery during the 1960s ("The Cargo Rap"); and the story of Irina, a Jewish
refugee from Poland who escaped the Nazis on a children's transport
to England, and Louis, a West Indian man Irina meets hours before he
is to return from London to the Caribbean, disillusioned with British
society ("Higher Ground"). *The Nature of Blood* follows an even more
winding path through space and time, exploring the Nazi persecution
of the Jews of Europe through the story of Eva Stern, a young German
Holocaust survivor; retelling the story of Othello, the Moorish general brought to Venice to wage war against the Turks; recounting the
story of a blood libel and the ensuing public execution of three Jews
in a town near Venice in the late fifteenth century; and following
the life of Stephan Stern, Eva's uncle, who left Germany in the 1930s
to help found the state of Israel, where in his old age he has a brief
encounter with Malka, an Ethiopian Jew suffering racism at the hands
of her white co-religionists.

Both novels invite the reader to detect thematic connections
between the discrete narratives about disparate characters in different
times and places which they juxtapose. In the case of *Higher Ground*,
which consists of three clearly demarcated, ostensibly self-contained
novellas, the book's subtitle, *A Novel in Three Parts*, encourages the
reader to read the three sections together and to uncover paral
lels between the lives of the individual protagonists. The title of
The Nature of Blood similarly suggests a basic continuity between
the narratives which it places alongside one another. As Rothberg
notes, it gestures at "a commonality that links the different stories as
essentially the same. A transhistorical racist imaginary obsessed with
purity of blood seems to unite the various Jewish and black victims
across time" (*Multidirectional Memory* 164). The extremely fragmented

structure of the text also prompts the reader to look for connections. The narrative strands that make up the novel are not divided into clearly marked sections or chapters, as in *Higher Ground*, but merge and mingle at an ever-accelerating pace. In the process of disentangling these closely interwoven storylines, the reader cannot help but reflect on what it is that unites them.

The numerous words, phrases, motifs, and themes that echo from one narrative to another in both *Higher Ground* and *The Nature of Blood* have been discussed at length by other critics. Rather than rehearsing them here, I will give just a few examples of links between black and Jewish experience from the two novels. In *Higher Ground*, one of the themes connecting the enslavement of Africans recounted in the first section, the plight of black convicts in 1960s America explored in the second section, and the Holocaust and its aftermath examined in the third section, is that of physical and/or psychological captivity. The connection is made explicit by the protagonist of the second section, who, in letters to his relatives and would-be legal representatives, constantly filters his own situation through the prisms of both the Holocaust and African American slavery. Rudy repeatedly uses Holocaust terminology to describe his own experience of incarceration, calling the prison in which he is kept "Belsen" (69; 84; 145); referring to the wardens as "the Gestapo Police" (127); and wondering, while being held in solitary confinement with 24-hour light, whether "in Nazi Germany they used to keep the lights on as a form of torture" (72). He also employs images of slavery to depict his detention, and black United States citizenship in general, as similar states of imprisonment. For example, he regards the United States as a "plantation society" (67; 90) in which emancipation has yet to happen. Having been released from the maximum-security wing into the main prison population, he writes: "Restrictions still apply, but to me they are as welcome and as liberal as the emancipation proclamation that we have yet to hear" (147). Rudy's current predicament and the past experience of slavery are linked most memorably in the deranged letter to his dead mother with which this section ends, which brings prison life and plantation atrocities together in a hallucinatory fusion.

In *The Nature of Blood*, the parallels suggested between different characters are even more numerous and conspicuous. For example, the experience of the black Ethiopian Jew Malka in the 1980s is subtly connected with that of the white German Jew Eva in the 1930s. Their departure from their respective homelands is described in strikingly similar terms. Malka speaks of being "herded...on to buses" and being "stored like thinning cattle" on the Israeli embassy compound, where she and the other Ethiopian Jews were left to "graz[e] on concrete" before being air-lifted to Israel (200). This image of people treated like cattle uncannily recalls Eva's description of the crowded boxcar trains in which she and her parents had been forced to travel, like animals, to the concentration camp. Moreover, Malka and Eva both meet with prejudice and suspicion in the foreign country—Israel in the case of the former, England in the case of the latter—in which they try to rebuild their lives after their respective ordeals. Two other characters whose lives closely parallel each other are Stephan Stern and the African general whom we recognize as Othello, though he is not actually named as such in the text. Both characters leave behind their homeland, a wife, and a child to start a new life in a different country. Each passes through the island of Cyprus, on the border between the East and the West, and forms a romantic attachment across the colour line. Moreover, each is deluded by a naive idealism: Stephan is disappointed to find that the new homeland for which he had fought as a young man and which he had imagined as a haven for "the displaced and the dispossessed" (5) is not free from exclusionary practices, and Othello similarly underestimates the forces of nationalism and racism militating against his dream of being accepted into Venetian society and beginning "a new life of peace" (174), although he, unlike Stephan, does not quite seem to have realized this yet when his narrative suddenly breaks off.

Difference and distance in *Higher Ground*

In establishing such links among the narratives, *Higher Ground* and *The Nature of Blood* appear to invite the reader to recognize a common human essence that persists across space and time: differences between people that may seem profound are revealed to be only skin-deep. The equation between distinct historical experiences which Phillips's juxtaposition of stories of black and Jewish suffering thus seems to effect has led to accusations that he is appropriating or usurping histories that are foreign to him to articulate his own (people's) distress.[4] What is often overlooked, though, is the extent to which the novels themselves criticize or problematize such an approach. For example, in *Higher Ground*, the metaphorical conception of history implicit in Rudy Williams's account does not go unchallenged. As we have seen, Rudy understands his own situation in terms of the historical experiences of Holocaust victims and African American slaves. He regards history as a hall of mirrors, a walk through which affords one endless possibilities for self-recognition. Rudy is far less interested in entering into an ethical relationship with historical others than in appropriating their experience to bolster his own claim to victimhood. His epistolary interactions with his relatives and sympathizers, all of whom he manages to alienate by self-righteously castigating them for their failure to live up to the radical political ideals that he himself has espoused, also betray a measure of ruthlessness. In a rare moment of self-criticism and humility, Rudy admits lacking the strength to love and to be kind, which, as he points out, involves "giving up not acquiring, opening doors not closing them, reaching out not holding back" (168–69). Through his life-long endeavour to shape both the past and the present in his own image, he has closed himself off from encounters with modes of existence and experience different from and irreducible to his own. The fact that Phillips follows his story with one of Jewish suffering—that of a Polish Jewish refugee who is haunted by memories of her family members who died in the Holocaust—can be seen as a rebuke of Rudy's self-serving and exploitative analogizing.

Also worth noting is the hesitant, indirect manner in which Phillips tackles the subject of the Holocaust in *Higher Ground*. The first two stories, which are written in the first person and use simultaneous or epistolary narration, are characterized by a sense of intimacy and immediacy that is absent in the third story, which uses third-person retrospective narration. Moreover, as Zierler has observed, the Jewish narrative stands out in that "it demonstrates a marked reticence about its very subject. Throughout 'Higher Ground,' Phillips shies away from directly depicting the Holocaust, enshrouding Irene's story in so much hazy description that one never really gets the same sense of her character and realness as one does for the protagonists of the first two parts" (61). While Zierler calls Irina's story "the weakest" of the three pieces on account of its oblique and circumspect treatment of the Holocaust (61), I subscribe to a more generous reading, which regards its not being fully imagined not as proof of writerly failure but as an implicit acknowledgement on the part of the writer of his own distance from the experience he describes. The remarkable restraint which the author shows in dealing with the Holocaust stands in stark contrast—and serves as a corrective—to Rudy's arrogation of imaginative control over this traumatic history.

Moreover, while *Higher Ground* encourages the reader to search for connections between the different histories it recounts, the novel actually stages "a series of missed encounters" between those histories (Rothberg, *Multidirectional Memory* 159). Rudy's overidentification with slaves and Holocaust victims, which traps him in "a rhetoric of absolute victimization that ultimately eliminates all agency" (Rothberg, *Multidirectional Memory* 161), can be regarded as one such missed encounter; the most obvious example, though, is the missed encounter between Irene and Lewis. Though attracted to Irene, Lewis decides to return home to the Caribbean, thus refusing Irene's offer of contact and solidarity. As Rothberg puts it, in *Higher Ground*, "black and Jewish histories do not actually intersect, but approach each other and then veer away asymptotically" (*Multidirectional Memory* 162).

Complex relations in *The Nature of Blood*

Black-Jewish relations remain a complex matter in *The Nature of Blood*, as is apparent from the stories of Othello and Stephan Stern. Othello, as represented in Phillips's novel, tragically lacks insight into his own situation, failing to see the similarities between his own precarious position and that of the ghettoized Jews in Venice.[5] In an essay in *The European Tribe* ironically titled "A Black European Success," in which he sketches his interpretation of Othello, Phillips points out that behind the imperial glory of Venice lay a pervasive racism and xenophobia: "Sixteenth-century Venetian society both enslaved the black and ridiculed the Jew" (15). Phillips's Othello visits the Jewish ghetto and is depressed by the squalid conditions in which the Jews are forced to live, but he makes no connection to his own situation. Though a Jewish scholar acts as an intermediary between Othello and Desdemona, suggesting the potential for connections between blacks and Jews as victims of European modernity, Othello fails to acknowledge the correspondences between their respective predicaments and learns very little from the Jews' experience of racism and ghettoization. Stephan Stern's brief affair with the black Ethiopian Jew Malka, which concludes the novel, also appears to offer a glimmer of hope, but is marred by incomprehension and prejudice. Few words are exchanged between them, and Stephan never learns the story of Malka's journey to Israel and the racism she and her family have experienced, a story which is offered to the reader in a series of interior monologues that are italicized and enclosed in parentheses. Stephan's and Malka's essential isolation and loneliness, a feature shared by all characters in *The Nature of Blood* (Ledent 137), is ultimately unrelieved. It even turns out that Stephan, for all his youthful idealism, is not free from xenophobic impulses himself (Nowak 124, 132). Lying in bed with Malka, an immigrant just like him, he reflects: "she belonged to another land. She might be happier there. Dragging these people from their primitive world into this one, and in such a fashion, was not a policy with which he had agreed. They belonged to another place" (211–12). The Zionist vision of togetherness and mutuality meets its limit, it seems, in the figure of the racial other.

These missed encounters indicate that *The Nature of Blood* does not assume an uncomplicated relationship between black and Jewish identities and histories. The fact that the differences—both formal and thematic—among the narratives that Phillips juxtaposes are at least as pronounced as the similarities further suggests that the novel rejects simple equations and straightforward analogies. As Stephen Clingman writes, "the echoes between the stories are suggestive rather than symmetrical, ... there are waves of connection but also of refraction, interference and shift. We might say therefore that there is a kind of oscillation and vibration among these stories, a displacement back and forth between the metonymic and metaphoric, in which the principle of recognition is at work, but not of simple reproduction or repetition" (160). In bringing together black and Jewish history, Zierler observes, Phillips "maintain[s] a pattern of asymmetry," thereby "safeguard[ing] their respective integrity and specificity": "He creates contiguity without direct correspondence, effecting comparison without displacement" (62–63).

The indirect approach to the Holocaust that characterizes *Higher Ground* is absent, however, in *The Nature of Blood*, or so it seems at first sight. While Phillips's treatment of Jewish history in the former novel is marked by respectful reticence, *The Nature of Blood* broaches the subject of the Holocaust head-on, ostensibly abandoning all restraint.

The central consciousness through which Phillips represents the Nazi persecution of the Jews in *The Nature of Blood* is not that of a refugee who has escaped the worst atrocities and hence has no first-hand experience of them, but that of a concentration camp inmate who turns out to have been a member of the *Sonderkommando* and thus an eye-witness of the horror. *The Nature of Blood* draws a psychologically convincing and deeply moving portrait of a Holocaust survivor, of which no less a writer than J. M. Coetzee has remarked: "pages of Eva's story seem to come straight from hell, striking one with appalling power" (39). This power derives at least in part from the experimental modes of representation which Phillips employs in these sections of the novel, which register the shocking and unassimilable nature of the traumatic historical events they portray in formal terms. Yet, while the novel appears to put the reader in close contact with the reality of the Holocaust, it continually reminds him or her of his or her, and the author's, own distance from Eva's experience through the use of intertextuality. The representation of the Holocaust that we are offered is filtered through a number of well-known literary and testimonial texts, most prominently Anne Frank's *The Diary of a Young Girl* (2000 [1947]), allowing Phillips to self-consciously signal his historical and cultural remove from, and his inevitably mediated mode of access to, the reality he represents.[6]

Moreover, the author thwarts easy identification with the Anne Frank story which he echoes by departing very markedly from his source text, thus estranging and unsettling the reader. In his version of the story, the protagonist does not die of typhus in Bergen-Belsen but survives the Holocaust, only to commit suicide in an English hospital a short time later. Eva's older sister, who, like Anne's, is called Margot, turns out to resemble the Anne we know from the diary much more closely than Eva herself. However, sent into hiding by her parents, Phillips's Margot is raped by the man who is sheltering her—clearly a very different character than the individuals who assisted the Frank family while they were in hiding—is arrested, and dies "on a cold grey morning in a country that was not her own" (174). As Anne Whitehead points out, the alternative versions of the Anne Frank story that the author provides in Eva and Margot are "both aimed at revising and challenging popular myths and misconceptions of Anne Frank's story which highlight a consistently optimistic voice" (107). If Eva's fate shows that "survival is not necessarily a happy ending," Margot's fate demonstrates that "not all of those who sheltered Jews were as selfless in their motivations as the helpers of the Secret Annexe" (107). Phillips also undermines redemptive, "feel-good" readings of the diary by radically revising its much-abused most famous line: "I still believe, in spite of everything, that people are truly good at heart" (Frank 329–30). Anne Frank's declaration of faith in the ultimate goodness of people is widely believed to be the last line of the diary, even though in reality it occurs much earlier and in the middle of entries about the cruelty of the world. The belief that the diary, like the play and film based on it, ends with this optimistic statement obscures the fact that the end of the diary—which cuts off abruptly—means the author's imminent death. As Bruno Bettelheim has pointed out,

> Her seeming survival through her moving statement about the goodness of men releases us effectively of the need to cope with the problems Auschwitz presents. That is why we are so relieved by her statement. It explains why millions loved play and movie, because while it confronts us with the fact that Auschwitz existed, it encourages us at the same time to ignore any of its implications. If all men are good at heart, there never really was an Auschwitz; nor is there any possibility that it may recur. (251)

Phillips, however, recasts Anne Frank's hopeful words to convey a message of utter despair which leaves no room for recuperation: "You see, Eva, in spite of everything that we have lost, they still hate us, and they will always hate us" (87). Such conspicuous departures from the original story puncture the reader's complacency and invite him or her to confront his or her own appropriative tendencies.

Trauma, diaspora, and incomparability

The Holocaust narrative in *The Nature of Blood* hardly stands alone in Phillips's œuvre in using intertextuality to signal distance or difference. One could also point, in *The Nature of Blood*, to the Othello narrative, which rewrites Shakespeare's play, and to the story of the Jews of Portobuffole, which is based on historical accounts explicitly mentioned in the acknowledgements. In *Higher Ground*, "Heartland" echoes Joseph Conrad's *Heart of Darkness*, J. M. Coetzee's *Waiting for the Barbarians,* and Wilson Harris's *Heartland;* "The Cargo Rap" has its roots in George Jackson's prison memoir *Soledad Brother;* and "Higher Ground" appears to be indebted to Jean Rhys's *Voyage in the Dark* (Ledent 76–77). The indirectness of Phillips's approach to both Jewish and black history can be connected to the traumatic nature of the diasporic condition shared by the two groups. As Rothberg points out, "at the limit, diaspora frustrates all forms of metaphoric identification because it is rooted in, or—better—uprooted by traumatic history" (*Multidirectional Memory* 169).

Cathy Caruth argues that there is no point in comparing different traumas in the sense of equating them with one another, as trauma is a fundamentally unknowable experience and therefore escapes the logic of analogy or metaphor. Different traumatic experiences can only be linked together in a productive and responsible manner, Caruth writes, if one is prepared to abandon analogical or metaphorical modes of thinking which inevitably erase difference:

> in the case of traumatic experience—experiences not of wholly possessed, fully grasped, or completely remembered events but, more complexly, of partially unassimilated or "missed" experiences—one cannot truly speak of comparison in any simple sense. How, indeed, can one compare what is not fully mastered or grasped in experience, or what is missed, in two separate situations? Such a linking of experiences is not exactly an analogy or metaphor, which would suggest the identification or equation of experiences, since analogy and metaphor are traditionally understood in terms of what has been or can be phenomenally perceived or made available to cognition; the linking of traumas, or the possibility of communication or encounter through them, demands a different model or a different way of thinking that may not guarantee communication or acceptance but may also allow for an encounter that retains, or does not fully erase, difference
>
> (*Unclaimed Experience* 124n.14)

If metaphorical connections always involve a measure of violence in that they elide the specificity of distinct traumatic experiences, metonymical links temper or counteract this violence, enabling less-appropriative encounters between different traumatic experiences. Phillips's "indirect, metonymic form of reference to unrepresentable extreme violence," then, not only is "a mark of the contingencies of diasporic geographies," but also signals "the disruptions of traumatic history" (Rothberg, *Multidirectional Memory* 170). His work seeks to move beyond the isolation imposed by trauma by letting multiple histories of suffering address one another without collapsing one into the other. Bearing out Caruth's claim that "trauma itself may provide the very link between cultures" ("Trauma and Experience" 11), it offers a compelling reflection on how such mnemonic connections are to be made for visions of cross-cultural solidarity and justice rather than discord and violence to arise from them.

8
Entangled Memories in Anita Desai's *Baumgartner's Bombay*

This chapter will examine the mnemonic connections established between the Holocaust and histories of (post)colonial suffering in Anita Desai's *Baumgartner's Bombay* (1998 [1988]), another novel which reflects and elicits a relational understanding of trauma. *Baumgartner's Bombay* recounts the tragic life and violent death of Hugo Baumgartner, a Jew who emigrates from Nazi Germany to India in the late 1930s, thus escaping the Holocaust in which his mother will be killed—or so we infer from the fact that the last sign of life he receives from her is a postcard sent from a Nazi concentration camp dated February 1941 (his father gassed himself to death before Baumgartner's departure following temporary detention in Dachau). However, he finds himself imprisoned as an enemy alien in a British internment camp for the length of the war. When finally released, he is delivered into the chaos and escalating violence of pre-Partition Calcutta. He flees to Bombay, where he spends the rest of his life, only to have Germany catch up with him in the end: in the late 1980s the elderly and impoverished Baumgartner is stabbed to death in his apartment by Kurt, a young German drug addict.

The novel alternates between scenes of Baumgartner's last hours, spread out in Chapters 1, 3, 5, and 7, and the story of his life, starting from his childhood in Berlin, which is told in the longer Chapters 2, 4, and 6. While they are not explicitly introduced as such, the even-numbered chapters effectively function as flashbacks, motivated by memories evoked in the preceding odd-numbered chapters. Thus, Baumgartner's encounter with the boy from Germany, described in Chapter 1, reminds him of his childhood, and is followed by the story of his childhood days in Berlin in Chapter 2. If Chapter 3 recounts how Baumgartner looks up his German expatriate friend Lotte and sits reminiscing with her about how they first met, Chapter 4 tells us the story of Baumgartner's arrival in India, his meeting with Lotte in Calcutta, and his imprisonment in the internment camp. In Chapter 5, Baumgartner takes Kurt home with him and tells him about the silver trophies that he won with the racehorse he and his friend Chimanlal owned together; Chapter 6 provides the story of Baumgartner's life in Bombay after the war, including his friendship with Chimanlal. Chapter 7, finally, tells the story of Baumgartner's murder. The interwoven present and past narratives are framed by brief opening and closing sections centring on Lotte: the opening section shows her fleeing from the scene of the murder, and the closing section finds her wailing in her own apartment with the wartime postcards from Baumgartner's mother spread out on the table before her.

Just as India seems like an unlikely setting for a Holocaust novel, so a Jewish refugee from Nazi Germany seems like an unlikely protagonist for a novel by an Indian writer. As Desai has explained in several interviews, her interest in the experience of a German immigrant in India derives in part from her multicultural family background. The daughter of a Bengali father and a non-Jewish German mother who had moved to India in the 1920s, she was raised in Old Delhi speaking Hindi and German at home and English at school. Her cosmopolitan upbringing clearly informs her work, much of which celebrates India's vast multiplicity of ethnicities, languages, and religions. This is also evident in *Baumgartner's Bombay*. Upon arriving in India, Baumgartner sees that "India was two worlds, or ten" (85). Struck by the country's diversity and linguistic profusion, he finds that he has to create his own hybrid language to be able to capture his experience of it: "Languages sprouted around him like tropical foliage and he picked words from it without knowing if they were English or Hindi or Bengali—they were simply words he needed: chai, khana, baraf, lao, jaldi, joota, chota, peg, pani, karma, soda, garee...what was this language he was wrestling out of the air, wrenching around to his own purposes? He suspected it was not Indian, but India's, the India he was marking out for himself" (92).

In her essay "A Coat of Many Colours," Desai makes it clear that she is contemptuous of "[t]hose purists who speak of the desirability of one language, one tradition, one culture" (221). Her distrust of chauvinism and nationalism stems from first-hand knowledge of the destructive potential of such impulses. As a ten-year-old child she witnessed the Hindu-Muslim violence that followed in the wake of the partition of British India into the separate nations of India and Pakistan. Her British and Muslim neighbours and schoolmates suddenly vanished, the Muslims in flight from Hindu violence and headed for Pakistan. As she has stated in an interview, the tumultuous events of 1947 left a deep impression on her: "probably the most traumatic event of my childhood was the 15th of August of 1947, when the British and Muslim populations disappeared overnight, bringing about the transformation of the old city I knew into the new city of the postpartition [sic] era" (qtd. in Pandit 153). Partition and the demise of India's pluralistic society has provided one of the major recurring themes of her fiction, including *Baumgartner's Bombay*.

Up until this novel, Desai's work had been concerned solely with the Indian aspect of her identity. However, she had long wanted to write a novel that would incorporate her mother's German heritage. What triggered *Baumgartner's Bombay* was an elderly Austrian Jew she had observed in the streets of Bombay begging for food for his cats. Following his death, Desai was asked to translate letters of his, which, being filled with endearments and everyday questions, at first seemed insignificant to her, but which, she later realized, were heavily censored correspondence from a Nazi concentration camp. As she explains in an interview, "These letters were all stamped with the same number. Later I read that Jews in concentration camps during the holocaust were allowed to write a certain number of letters, during the early years at least. These letters were stamped with the numbers they bore in the camps. Only then did I realize what that number had meant" (qtd. in Pandit 156). Following this revelation, she started to imagine the man's absent story: "Because there was no information about them [the letters] the man was dead, I couldn't question him—I began to think a great deal about it and felt the need to supply them with a history, so I invented a history for this figure whom I had seen but not known" (qtd. in Jussawalla 175). Feeling compelled to invent a possible history for the man who had died, she drew on her mother's stories about pre-war Germany, on Holocaust literature, on written documents about internment camps for enemy aliens in England and Canada during the Second World War, and on oral accounts of the internment camp experience in India to write *Baumgartner's Bombay*.[1] Desai recognizes that "[i]t is the first time [she] ever wrote about a character who was not Indian," and that in so doing she "seem[s] to have taken a step outside [her] own area of experience" (qtd. in Pandit 164).

It is worth noting, however, that Desai's evocation of the Holocaust—which the protagonist escapes and in which his mother dies—hardly strays beyond the bounds of her own experience. After all, *Baumgartner's Bombay* does not actually represent the Nazi genocide, though its presence is felt throughout the novel, from the first page to the last. Its most powerful trace is the bundle of postcards that Lotte rescues from Baumgartner's apartment, which obviously recalls the letters sent to the Austrian Jew that Desai had translated. They are cards from Baumgartner's mother, each stamped with the number "J 673/1," presumably the number she bore in the Nazi concentration camp where she was being held. As was the case with the letters, the postcards, which merely repeat the same empty phrases, appear to be all but meaningless to Lotte: "She read on and each line seemed like the other, each card alike: 'Are you well, my rabbit? Do not worry yourself. I am well. I have enough. But have you enough, my mouse, my darling? Do not worry...' " (3). While they lack meaningful content, for the simple reason that concentration camp inmates were allowed to say very little, their very existence, and the fact that they stop abruptly, is of course hugely significant: indeed, it bears silent witness to horrors which they do not describe. Thus, the impact of the postcards depends heavily on the reader's historical knowledge of the Holocaust. Just as Caryl Phillips signals his historical and cultural remove from the reality of the Holocaust through the use of intertextuality in the narrative of Eva Stern, so Desai maintains a respectful distance from it by adopting this indirect approach. While showing "the utmost discretion" in her handling of the Holocaust, Desai does not allow the reader to forget this pivotal event for a single moment, as Baumgartner's character and personality turn out to have been profoundly shaped by it (Furst 173). Haunted by survivor guilt and "traumatized into a belief in his own powerlessness to direct his own life in any way," Baumgartner becomes an isolated, detached, and lonely figure, wary of relationships with others that might lead to more hurt, and passively accepts and endures whatever life throws at him (Furst 173).

The author's personal background as a product of cultural mixing gives her a double perspective which, as Bryan Cheyette puts it, "enables [her] to view Indian history through European eyes and European history through Indian eyes" ("Venetian Spaces" 68). With Aamir Mufti, I believe that the novel's project can best be described as an attempt to excavate "a subterranean history ... of the modern world, a network of subterranean and uncanny linkages that connect 'Europe' to the world's 'peripheries' " (249). Through the figure of the Jewish refugee it identifies forms and practices of what Paul Gilroy, in *Between Camps*, calls "camp-thinking" wherever and whenever they manifest themselves in the modern era. "Camp-thinking" refers to the division of people into sharply polarized, rigid, and exclusive camps, whether on racial, ethnic, national, cultural, or religious grounds. These can be literal camps—refugee camps, concentration camps, or internment camps—but also metaphorical camps. Camp-thinking fosters totalizing and essentialist conceptions of identity that, in turn, lead to exclusionary politics. Desai's novel not only observes the pervasiveness of racial and other absolutisms, but it also resists the myopic logic that can comprehend the sufferings of different victim groups only in particularistic terms (Gilroy, *Between Camps* 80). It links multiple historical traumas together, making them resonate with and echo one another. As will become apparent, mirroring, copying, and repeating are important motifs throughout the text, which are used to dislodge the Holocaust from its spatial and temporal moorings, and to connect worldwide instances of violence and intolerance against "other" peoples who are denied a sense of belonging to the national community.

While the novel's protagonist views history fatalistically as "Endless war. Eternal war" (180) and "A great web in which each one was trapped, a nightmare from which one could not emerge" (173), it seems to me that *Baumgartner's Bombay* is not content to offer a tragic vision of history as an endlessly recurring nightmare. The text asks to be read, I argue, not as a lesson in fatalism but as a cautionary tale about the dangers of camp-thinking. As we will see, the novel makes a point of noting how the characters are oblivious to the connections between their own and other people's histories of victimization—indeed, they tend to be too preoccupied with their own troubles to take an interest in what goes on elsewhere in the world, let alone to care about it. In fact, this self-absorption is precisely what *Baumgartner's Bombay* denounces, as it is generative of camp-thinking, exclusionary politics, and, ultimately, violence and oppression. Desai's repeated insistence on the lack of engagement with and disregard for others shown by the characters can be interpreted as an implicit call for transcultural remembrance, which might serve as an antidote to pessimism, despair, and defeatism.

Circular movements

The novel's concern with repetition and circularity is already signalled by its epigraph, taken from T. S. Eliot's poem "East Coker":

> In my beginning is my end. In succession
> Houses rise and fall, crumble, are extended,
> Are removed, destroyed, restored...

The epigraph is borne out by the circular structure of the novel. The end of *Baumgartner's Bombay* is indeed in its beginning, as it both opens and concludes with Lotte's despair over Baumgartner's murder. However, circular movements are particularly evident and significant on the level of plot, as the trajectory of Baumgartner's life turns out to be singularly marked by repetition. For example, there is a cruel irony implicit in the fact that Baumgartner, who has come to India to be safe from Nazi persecution, is murdered there half a century later by a young "Aryan" German. The killer is a supremely selfish countercultural tourist, whom Baumgartner has taken home after finding him slumped with no money in a local restaurant where Baumgartner is a regular. He does so at the request of the owner, Farrokh, who assumes that Baumgartner and Kurt share a kinship since they are both *firanghis* (foreigners) linked by language. Kurt repays Baumgartner for his kindness by killing him for the silver trophies won by the racehorse he had once owned, thus continuing the work of the Nazis and bringing the elderly Jew's life full circle.[2] In fact, Baumgartner has a sense of foreboding about their chance encounter right from the start. Immediately recognizing him as a German, Baumgartner perceives the boy as a reincarnation of the Nazi spirit even before any exchange has taken place between them.

Their meeting sets off a chain of memories that takes him back to the horrors of the past:

> That fair hair, that peeled flesh and the flash on the wrist—it was a certain type that Baumgartner had escaped, forgotten. Then why had this boy to come after him, in lederhosen [sic], in marching boots, striding over the mountains to the sound of the *Wandervogels Lied*? The *Lieder* and the campfire. The campfire and the beer. The beer and the yodelling. The yodelling and the marching. The marching and the shooting. The shooting and the killing. The killing and the killing and the killing. (21)

Through a series of metonymic links, Baumgartner connects the boy in Bombay with the Nazi camps which he had escaped but in which his mother died. Plagued by survivor guilt, he seems to know that he has met his own end as soon as he sees the boy, and he almost welcomes it. Being murdered at the hands of a German, like his mother, is a way of erasing the guilt he feels for having survived the Holocaust, unlike so many others.

In an interview with Feroza Jussawalla, Desai reveals that in writing the book she considered two alternative endings, the one we know and one in which Baumgartner would have been murdered by the beggar living outside the door of his apartment building, and that she settled on the former because of its greater tragic potential. Asked why she decided to have her protagonist killed off by a German hippie, Desai replies:

> It's something which worried me extremely. Although I knew he would die in the end, I had no idea who was going to kill him, and right through the book I was playing with two alternative endings. The other person who could have killed him was that beggar who lives on the street in front of his house, in whose eyes Baumgartner is wealthy. He could easily have robbed him and killed him. I had, in fact, written two alternative endings for that book. One was his murder by this beggar, but that dissatisfied me because that was simply random violence, it was the kind of murder which does take place in big cities. It had no real meaning and Baumgartner was left incomplete or unfulfilled in a certain sense, because all through he has a sense of having escaped death

in Germany. His mother was killed but he escaped. The reason for his sadness through the book is this death that he escaped so that it pursues him and stalks him right through the book. I had to have it catch up with him in the end, and it seemed right and jus-tified in the Greek sense if that death would be death by a Nazi, by a German. That gave me a certain satisfaction, that he had met the kind of death that fate had devised for him anyway. He had fooled fate for awhile and escaped for awhile, but in the end it got him.

(qtd. in Jussawalla 176)

Apart from making for a satisfactorily tragic ending, the explicit affin-ity between Kurt and the Nazis that killed Baumgartner's mother points to a continuity between contemporary Germany and the Holocaust. Kurt's apparent lack of awareness of, or indifference to, the history that has led Baumgartner to move to India, together with the fact that after the murder he escapes arrest, reinforces the damn-ing criticism of contemporary Germany's handling of its wartime past which this episode can be seen to contain. The rejection by the postwar generation of the values and beliefs of the previous genera-tion that lived through and fought the Second World War, which is implied by Kurt's countercultural relationship to India, amounts to empty posturing and involves an evasion of historical responsibility (Mufti 250).

If the manner of Baumgartner's death suggests that the Holocaust is an unresolved history, another ironic repetition brings to light uncanny similarities between Nazism and the policies and ideolo-gies of those fighting on the other side. After narrowly avoiding the Nazi concentration camps, where he would inevitably have ended up had he stayed in Germany like his mother, Baumgartner is arrested in India as an enemy alien and, along with all other German nation-als, imprisoned in a British internment camp for the length of the war. Thus, both mother and son spend the war in a camp, the for-mer for being a Jew in Germany, the latter for being a German in India. Baumgartner's plea to be released goes unheeded, as the British make no distinction between "Aryan" Germans who support the Nazi government and German Jews who have come to India to escape persecution under that very regime. In a further irony, the internment camp begins to resemble Nazi Germany, to the point of becoming "an extension" of it (116), as the British authorities allow the Nazis among the inmates to occupy positions of power in the camp and to impose on the Jewish internees the same forms of authority to which they would have been subjected back home in Germany. A strict physical regime is established, they find themselves forced into public displays of loyalty to Germany, and their mail disappears. Baumgartner's immediate impression that the British camp guard who imposes barracks discipline on the German inmates and their self-appointed leaders "were of a kind—the ruling kind" (104) further underscores the affinity between British imperialism and Nazi domination. So does a remark the British camp commander makes upon being informed that the Jewish inmates have been beaten up by the Nazis in the camp for refusing to comply with the rules imposed on them (saluting the flag, shouting "Heil Hitler," etc.): "Why is everyone so excited? This happens all the time in our public schools. It doesn't mean much—just a thrashing" (117). His reaction suggests that this kind of conduct is common practice in Britain as well: it is not just the Nazis who behave in this way; the British do it too, and they even consider it normal and acceptable. As Mufti points out, "One consequence of this displacing of German fascism to colonial soil is the insertion of the British into its problematic, therefore removing the former from within the confines of a single nation-state and restoring to it the horizon of (European) modernity as a whole" (253). The continuities between Nazism and British imperialism were also noted by India's future prime minister Jawaharlal Nehru, who, writing in prison during the Second World War, argued that "we in India have known racialism in all its forms ever since the commencement of British rule. The whole ideology of this rule was that of the herrenvolk [sic] and the master race, and the structure of government was based upon it" (qtd. in Mufti 6).

Baumgartner's release from the internment camp at the end of the war does not make for a clean break with the troubled European past, as the soon-to-be-independent India into which he emerges is hardly a stranger to exclusionary, blood-and-soil-type nationalisms. Having been isolated from the world around him during his imprisonment, Baumgartner is baffled to find war raging in the streets of Calcutta, as the country in which he had sought refuge prepares for Independence and Partition. The division of the Indian subcontinent along religious lines into the independent states of India and

Pakistan in 1947 forced an estimated 14.5 million Hindus, Muslims, and Sikhs to flee their homes and led to the violent deaths of up to one million people. The large-scale ethnic violence and mass migration that accompanied Partition are represented in Desai's novel through the stories of two characters in particular: Baumgartner's neighbour Sushil, who is brutally murdered by Hindu extremists, presumably for political reasons, and his Muslim business partner Habibullah, who finds himself forced to flee from Calcutta to Dacca and is never heard from again. Though the novel refrains from drawing direct analogies, the ethnic cleansing of Partition clearly echoes the Nazi policies of racial purification that drove Baumgartner out of Germany and resulted in his mother's death. In a telling instance of multidirectional memory, Baumgartner unconsciously connects the murder of Sushil to the death of his mother: "When he climbed up to the loft and called, 'Sushil? Sushil?' he saw the radio buff's chair overturned and the boy lying face down on the floor. The blood streamed. . . . In his sleep, in his dreams, the blood was Mutti's, not the boy's. Yet his mother—so small, weak—could not have spilt so much blood. Or had she? The blood ran, ran over the floor and down the stairs, soaking his feet which stood in it helplessly" (179).

Baumgartner dreams that the blood shed by a victim of Partition violence is the blood of his mother, who died in the Holocaust. In fact, a further connection is suggested with Baumgartner's own murder, which similarly involves someone standing in a pool of blood—Kurt—and leaving bloody footprints on the stairs and the floor of the hall as he flees the scene (220–21). In another link between the Holocaust and Partition, uncertainty surrounds the fate of both Baumgartner's mother and Habibullah. In both cases Baumgartner, and with him the reader, is left in the dark as to what has befallen them: he has no conclusive proof that they have been killed, only circumstantial evidence. In fact, as Baumgartner comes to understand what has in all likelihood happened to his mother after belatedly receiving her postcards, the narrator observes that "[t]he Calcutta he lived in now—the Calcutta that had seen the famine of 1943, that had prepared for a Japanese attack, that had been used and drained by the war and war profiteers and now prepared for the great partition—was the proper setting for his mourning" (165–66). This striking claim, that Partition-era India is a proper setting for

mourning the Holocaust, dispels any impression the reader might
have had that the novel's conjoining of India and the Nazi genocide
is incongruous or gratuitous. What *Baumgartner's Bombay* suggests
through this conjunction is that the persecution of the European Jews
under Nazism resonates on a fundamental level with the oppression
of ethnic minorities elsewhere in the world, such as India's Muslim
population at the time of Partition (Mufti 255).

On Habibullah's advice, Baumgartner leaves the riot-filled streets
of Calcutta for the relative safety of Bombay, where he will live out
the rest of his life. However, he is never allowed to feel at home there
either. If to the Nazis in Germany he was a Jew and to the British in
India a German, to those he meets and deals with in his everyday life
in India he is and will always remain a foreigner, even though he has
traded in his German passport for an Indian one: "He had lived in
this land for fifty years—or if not fifty then so nearly as to make no
difference—and it no longer seemed fantastic and exotic; it was more
utterly familiar now than any landscape on earth. Yet the eyes of the
people who passed by glanced at him who was still strange and unfa-
miliar to them, and all said: *Firanghi*, foreigner" (19). The ultimate
outsider, Baumgartner not only has to flee Germany as he becomes
"unacceptable" there, but he is never fully accepted in his country
of refuge either: "Accepting—but not accepted; that was the story of
his life, the one thread that ran through it all. In Germany he had
been dark—his darkness had marked him the Jew, *der Jude*. In India
he was fair—and that marked him the *firanghi*. In both lands, the
unacceptable" (20). Even the landscape appears to reject him. While
travelling for business, Baumgartner explores what appears to be a
sacred cave. All of a sudden he has a powerful sensation of being
expelled from there, which reminds him of his rejection in Germany
as a Jew:

> He turned and scrambled out of the narrow exit with such speed
> that he scratched his arms against the stone, hurt his knee against
> its rib, and fell out on to the hillside as if ejected by what-
> ever possessed or inhabited that temple. Indigestible, inedible
> Baumgartner. The god had spat him out. *Raus*, Baumgartner, out.
> Not fit for consumption, German or Hindu, human or divine.
>
> Half-way down the track, laughing in humiliation and mortifi-
> cation as he rubbed his scratched elbows, Baumgartner knew he

had been expelled from some royal presence. Go, Baumgartner. Out. He had not been found fit. Shabby, dirty white man, *firanghi,* unwanted. *Raus,* Baumgartner, *raus.* (190)

The cave episode—a reprise of the Marabar Caves incident in E. M. Forster's *A Passage to India* (1924)—confirms Baumgartner's inability to fit in anywhere. The social exclusion he experiences as a European in post-Independence India reduces him to poverty, as he finds it impossible to find employment after the death of his Hindu business partner Chimanlal, his only Indian friend. The deteriorating circumstances of Baumgartner's life in India thus repeat the decline of his family's fortunes in 1930s Germany. Hence, the title of the novel has an ironic ring to it: echoing the titles of popular travel guides (such as *Baedeker's Egypt* or *Fodor's Tokyo*), it promises access to a different world, but Baumgartner's Bombay turns out to be depressingly similar to the Berlin of his childhood. Like Germany, India oppresses its minorities and reduces him to poverty; moreover, he ends up being killed there by a German, just as he would have been had he stayed in Germany. Another stroke of irony is that the title suggests ownership, whereas in reality Baumgartner is constantly made to feel that he does not belong there.

In fact, the only place where Baumgartner has ever felt at home is the city of Venice, which he passed through on his way from Germany to India. An outsider in the East as well as in the West, he is most comfortable in the transitional space between East and West that is both and neither: "Venice *was* the East, and yet it was Europe too; it was that magic boundary where the two met and blended, and for those seven days Hugo had been a part of their union. He realised it only now: that during his constant wandering, his ceaseless walking, he had been drawing closer and closer to this discovery of that bewitched point where they became one land of which he felt himself the natural citizen" (63). Many years later Baumgartner still fondly remembers his time in Venice, which he imagines to be a place "between camps." When Lotte at one point tells him that there is no home for the two of them, he replies: "If I could go, if I could leave, then I would go to Venice.... Once I was there—for seven days. I caught the boat to India from there. It was so strange—it was both East and West, both Europe and Asia. I thought—maybe, in such a place, I could be at home" (81). Baumgartner mentions Venice once again when Kurt, after finishing his monologue about the various places he has visited, asks him where he has been and what he has seen: "Once—when I was a young fellow—many years ago—I was in Venice. *Ja*, seven days I have in Venice once. Ah, Venice.... It was wonderful. *Es war prima*" (160). Baumgartner's image of Venice seems to be somewhat naive or romantic, especially compared to the bleak picture presented by Phillips in *The European Tribe* and *The Nature of Blood*. After all, Phillips makes it clear that—historically, at least—Venice does marginalize, exclude, and discriminate against outsiders, such as blacks and Jews. Baumgartner has the most fleeting of encounters with a Jewish woman there, but he never quite manages to enter the Jewish ghetto and to join the Jewish community in Venice—indeed, he gets lost on the way there (62–63). However, even if he had found the Jewish ghetto and settled down there, it is doubtful that he would have lived happily ever after, as more than two hundred Jews were deported from there to the Nazi death camps in 1943 and 1944. It would appear, then, that the city in which Baumgartner dreams of being at home is an idyllic haven only within the confines of his imagination.[3]

The novel establishes further links between Baumgartner's precarious situation in India and the predicament of rural migrants living in abject poverty on the streets of Bombay, another group which does not fully belong to the national community:

There seemed to be a drought every year in the land and the pavement filled visibly with a migrant population from the fields and villages. One family had taken up the length of the pavement just outside Hira Niwas. Overnight their tins, rags, ropes, strings, papers and plastic bags had been set up to make a shelter and when the tenants woke next morning, they found a cooking fire burning, tin pots and pans being washed in the gutter and some were actually witnesses to the birth of a new baby on a piece of sacking in the street. The doorman, himself a migrant but an earlier one, driven here by an earlier calamity, now possessor of a job and an official status and therefore infinitely superior to them, yet not so superior as to run no risk of contamination from the starved and the luckless, cursed them from his safe perch in the doorway, and the tenants stopped on their way in or out to express their horror and contempt for the ragged creatures who hardly seemed human to the citizens of the *urbis et prima* of the west. (207)

The street people's extreme poverty recalls the impoverishment of the German Jews in the late 1930s. The family on the pavement is similarly despised by Baumgartner's better-off Indian neighbours; Baumgartner himself, however, feels not contempt but shame: "Baumgartner, for one, shuffled past with his head bowed and his eyes averted—not to avoid contamination as the others did, but to hide his shame at being alive, fed, sheltered, privileged" (207). After all, he has been in their shoes—or other German Jews have, in any case. Baumgartner's own family did not live in abject poverty in the late 1930s, but many other Jews did: "they were not as poor as others were. Unlike the men who searched the dustbins for chicken bones and slept on benches under sheets of *Berliner Zeitung*, or the women who stood on the streets because there was nowhere else to go, their scent reeking of cheapness, the Baumgartners did not starve" (40). Moreover, this could easily have been his own fate in Bombay if he had not had the extraordinary good fortune of being offered a job by Chimanlal: after all, no one else would have hired him. Baumgartner's experience resonates particularly with that of the street woman, who is a victim not only of economic deprivation but also of domestic violence. His suffering and his inability to change his situation are mirrored by her passive endurance of her husband's abuse.

Cross-cultural incomprehension

The characters themselves, however, appear by and large to be oblivious to the resonances outlined above—which is part of the problem the novel diagnoses. Baumgartner's repeated victimization results from his being treated not as a unique individual but as a representative of one group or another—Jews, Germans, or *firanghis*—upon whom a devalued identity is conferred, leading to their marginalization, exclusion, or elimination. At several points, the novel highlights the ignorance of the Indian characters about the Holocaust. Habibullah, for example, despite being a close colleague, turns out to be unaware of Baumgartner's national or ethnic background and to have no knowledge of what has happened in Europe:

> "How? Are you not English, European *sahib*? Have you no European connections? You can help him with export business—"

"Europe has had a war, Habibullah," Baumgartner reminded him. "My country is—finished. What business can I do?"

But Habibullah had no more conception of Baumgartner's war, of Europe's war than Baumgartner had of affairs in Bengal, in India. (169)

Farrokh, the proprietor of the Café de Paris, displays a similar kind of blindness. Aware that Baumgartner and Kurt are from the same country and speak the same language, he assumes that this link between them will oblige Baumgartner to take responsibility for Kurt: "Mr Baumgartner, what can I do? Please tell me—there is man from your country.... That is only reason why I fed him... I know you, I know your country must be good country, so I gave food to the boy. Then he no pay" (139). Clearly, Farrokh does not realize that Baumgartner and Kurt are on opposite sides of an old conflict between different communities within Germany, nor does he understand why Baumgartner might strongly disagree with Farrokh's description of his homeland as a "good country." Farrokh's blindness is a fatal repetition of the blindness displayed by the British, who detained German Jews and Nazis together during the war. Another Indian character that fails to make such crucial distinctions is Baumgartner's neighbour Sushil, an Indian nationalist and Marxist turned radio mechanic:

The day he discovered that Baumgartner was German, he lit up with admiration as if in the presence of a war hero. "But a Jew, a Jew, not a Nazi," Baumgartner tried to deflect the misplaced ardour but this meant nothing to Sushil who had renounced religion for politics and had no interest in Judaism; nor would he entertain any criticism of the German regime. "If they had defeated the British, then they would have helped Japan to drive them out of India. They are our friends, Japan and Germany." When Baumgartner stammered that they were not his friends, Sushil politely changed the subject, saying, "Now I am not so political, now I want to learn other things." (177)

By showing that the Holocaust is not a major concern of people in India, if they are aware of it at all, the novel can be seen to challenge the rash generalizations made by scholars such as Daniel

Levy and Natan Sznaider or Jeffrey Alexander, who, as we saw in Chapter 6, claim that the Holocaust has become a global, universal, or cosmopolitan memory that guarantees human rights and offers humanity a moral foundation.

However, the Indian characters certainly have no monopoly on ignorance about and disinterest in the traumas of others. Though Baumgartner sees himself as infinitely accepting and accommodating of others, he turns out to be a case in point of the tendency towards self-absorption, the lack of curiosity about and concern for the unique individuality of other people that the text holds up to critical scrutiny. After all, he views all those around him simply as "Indians," just as they view him as another *firanghi*: "Muslims killed Hindus, Hindus Muslims. Baumgartner could not fathom it— to him they were Indians seen in a mass and, individually, Sushil the Marxist, Habibullah the trader" (180). Seeing his Indian acquaintances in isolation from their religious background, Baumgartner no more comprehends Habibullah's reasons for fleeing to the newly created East Pakistan than the latter comprehends why the former cannot simply resume his pre-war life. Having listened only to the overseas news while in the camp, Baumgartner is unaware of what is happening in India. Hence, he is puzzled by Habibullah's response to his suggestion that business will surely go on now that the war is over: "Not for me, *sahib*, not for my family. For us—India is finished. Don't you know, every night they come and threaten us in our house? Every night they set some Muslim house on fire, stab some Muslim in the street, rob him too. Don't you know, *sahib*, they are driving us out?" (168). When Baumgartner, confused, asks him who "they" are, Habibullah patiently explains: "These—these Congresswallahs, *sahib*, the Hindus ... They say they will kick out the British. Even the British are saying they will leave. And this man Jinnah, and his party—they are wanting partition, they are also wanting to leave. All Muslims should leave, they say. But—how? I have so much—my family, my home, my business—what will happen to it all, *sahib*?" (168). As Efraim Sicher and Linda Weinhouse note, "Desai introduces an explicit parallel between the fate of European Jews and the fate of Muslims in post-colonial India and shows how difficult it is for each group to imagine the other's reality" (22).[4]

Not only does Baumgartner see Indians as a homogeneous mass of people, resulting in an inability to understand the Hindu-Muslim conflict, but his perception of India, like that of the other European characters, is also strongly coloured by orientalist stereotypes. India is seen as exotic, primitive, barbaric, and inferior: a kind of counter-image of Western modernity. The exoticization of India starts well before Baumgartner arrives there. As Bryan Cheyette points out, Desai plays with the idea of German orientalism from the beginning of the narrative: orientalist images of India are already very prominent in the chapter on Baumgartner's childhood in Germany ("Venetian Spaces" 69). Herr Pfuehl, who is intent on laying his hands on the Baumgartners' ornate furniture shop (made up, among other things, of "Empire suites" [26]), describes India as "an ancient and back-ward land,...the land of snakes and fakirs," which is redeemed only by the fact that it is "a colony of our neighbours in Britain" (53). Baumgartner's mother's cult of the Bengali poet Tagore shows how India inspires fascination in Europeans: Tagore is described by a friend of Baumgartner's mother as "a strange Indian poet" (47) with "hypnotic eyes" (48), and his mother is said to be "entranced" while listening to her friend talk about him (48). However, when Baumgartner attempts to persuade his mother to come to India with him by saying that "[a]fter all, they are not so primitive" (55) and reminding her of the great poet Tagore, she counters: "Ach Hugo, don't be ridiculous. Why should your mother read a *bengalische* poet when I can read the beautiful verses of our dear Friedmanns?" (56). This rhetorical question indicates that she considers even the best Indian poetry to be inferior to the German amateur rhyme penned by her friends. She cannot imagine herself living in "some dangerous land in the East, *mit den Schwarzen*" (57) and refuses to accompany her son, even though her living conditions in Germany are very harsh.

The outlook of the European characters does not fundamentally change when they arrive in India. Indeed, they view the country and its **inhabitants** in a distinctly unflattering, demeaning man-ner. Patrick Hogan points out that throughout the novel the Indian masses are "unindividuated and inscrutable" (41). In the novel's opening sentence, they appear to Lotte as a "collected crowd of identical individuals" (1), and Baumgartner, upon his arrival in Bombay, perceives them as "one restless, heaving mass" (83). More-over, the Indian people are referred to through "metaphors of animals and vermin" (Hogan 41): for example, the Indians with whom Baumgartner shares a building in Calcutta are said to form "families that lived in the cracks and crevices of the building like so many rats, or lice" (174). Furthermore, the sight of Indian peasants leads Baumgartner to marvel at their supposedly simple, primitive, and history-less lives: "When he overcame and left behind his initial horror at the sight of women carrying excreta on their heads, and digging their hands into it as they might into wet dough or laundry, and his initial bewilderment at lives so primitive, so basic and unchanging, he began to envy them that simplicity, the absence of choice and history" (111). The European characters also think of Hinduism as a form of primitive, barbaric idolatry. Baumgartner wonders whether the cave temple was "the scene of some hideous human sacrifice" and conjures up visions of "cannibalistic rites" (190). Kurt's recollection, or fantasy, of cannibalism is an even more striking instance of this association of Hindu rituals and practices with savagery (Hogan 43). Focusing on the most exotic, bizarre, and lugubrious aspects of Indian culture, Kurt's account of his trip is a "flood of repetitive Indian horror stories, involving cannibalism, ritual sacrifice, wholesale slaughter, leprosy, flagellation, excess both erotic and narcotic, and finally, farcically, a yeti" (Newman).

The catalogue of orientalist stereotypes that we find in *Baumgartner's Bombay* has led some critics to accuse the novel of complicity in colonial ideology. Tony da Silva, for example, takes offence at "the cruel and unsympathetic picture of India and its people" presented in Desai's novel, which, in his view, effectively "legitimize[s] a discourse of complete negation in which India is not modern, not developed, not civilized, not Western." According to Hogan, who shares da Silva's assessment, the problem is compounded by the novel's connection to Joseph Conrad's *Heart of Darkness* (2006 [1902]), a novella which has been interpreted—most famously by Chinua Achebe—as dehumanizing non-white people and denigrating their culture. As Hogan convincingly demonstrates (36–45), Desai draws on Conrad's novella to a very large extent in *Baumgartner's Bombay*, arguably making it the novel's primary intertext. She borrows the general narrative of a European adventurer entering non-European territory but shifts the latter from Africa to Asia. In *Heart of Darkness*, Kurtz travels to the heart of Africa in search of ivory, mingles with the natives, is drawn into the local savagery, goes half-mad, falls ill, and is nursed by another European voyager, the Russian trader. Desai's character Kurt, whose name echoes Conrad's Kurtz, travels to the heart of India in search of drugs, becomes involved with the local savagery, loses his physical and mental health, and is taken care of by Baumgartner. Kurt's murder of Baumgartner for his silver trophies, which will allow him to buy more heroin, recalls Kurtz's threat to the Russian trader that he will kill him if the Russian refuses to give Kurt his ivory. However, Baumgartner is modelled not only on the Russian but also on Marlow, the narrator-protagonist of *Heart of Darkness*. As Hogan points out, Baumgartner plays the role of Marlow in relation to Farrokh, who is the counterpart of the company manager in *Heart of Darkness* (39). Just like the latter, Farrokh aims to rid himself and his business of Kurt/Kurtz, fearing that trade will suffer, and appeals to Baumgartner/Marlow to assist him in this matter.

Apart from similarities at the level of plot and character, there are also a significant number of parallel incidents, scenes, images, and phrases in *Baumgartner's Bombay* and *Heart of Darkness*. A good example is provided by the scene of Baumgartner travelling on a steamship to Dacca:

> Baumgartner on the steamship, travelling to Dacca. Baumgartner with his feet sweating in white canvas shoes, propped up on the rail, sitting in the shade of a straw hat and studying the bank in an attempt at separating the animate from the inanimate. The forest that was like a shroud on the bank, ghostly and impenetrable. Crocodiles that slept like whitened stones, spattered by the excrement of the egrets that rode them delicately. Bamboos that stirred, women who lowered brass pots into the muddy swirl from which a fish leapt suddenly—but when he remembered them later, in a hotel room in a steaming city that rang with rickshaw bells, he wondered if it had not all been a mirage, a dream. If it had been a real scene, in a real land, then Baumgartner with his hat and shoes would have been too unlikely a visitor to be possible, a hallucination for those who watched from the shore. If he were real, then surely the scene, the setting was not. How could the two exist together in one land? The match was improbable beyond belief. (92–93)

This scene not only recalls Marlow's steamboat voyage up the Congo river but also his meditations on the impenetrable darkness of the African forest and on its dream-like, hallucinatory quality. The constant use of negative modifiers in this passage ("impenetrable," "unlikely," and "improbable") and elsewhere in the novel is a clear echo from *Heart of Darkness*, where Marlow, finding himself unable to precisely relate his experience of Africa, resorts to the same kind of rhetoric. To give but one example from Conrad's novella: "His [the Russian's] very existence was improbable, inexplicable, and altogether bewildering. He was an insoluble problem. It was inconceivable how he had existed, how he had succeeded in getting so far, how he had managed to remain—why he did not instantly disappear" (54). In another scene that appears to have been borrowed from *Heart of Darkness*, Baumgartner is baffled by the restraint shown by the people living on the pavement outside his building, who could easily rob him of his possessions yet have never done so: "Although he barely acknowledged this to himself, it was true that he had fears—nightmares—of their coming after him one night. Why should they not? They saw him bring bags of food, knew he had a wallet in his pocket, wore a watch on his wrist, good shoes on his feet...and he wondered what prevented them from grabbing him by his neck and stripping him in the dark" (145). In *Heart of Darkness*, Marlow similarly marvels over what stops the hungry cannibals on his steamer from killing and eating the European crew members, whom they vastly outnumber: "Why in the name of all the gnawing devils of hunger they didn't go for us—they were thirty to five—and have a good tuck-in for once, amazes me now when I think of it.... Restraint! What possible restraint? Was it superstition, disgust, patience, fear—or some kind of primitive honour?... Restraint! I would just as soon have expected restraint from a hyena prowling amongst the corpses of a battlefield" (41–42). Also reminiscent of *Heart of Darkness* is the aforementioned scene of Baumgartner standing helplessly in Sushil's blood, whose multidirectionality is thus even more striking than previously noted: it resonates not only with the death of Baumgartner's mother and his own murder, but also with the scene from Conrad's novella in which "a pool of blood" oozes around Marlow's shoes after the African helmsman has been killed by a spear (46).

Desai's revision of Conrad's novella does not find favour with Hogan, who accuses the author of uncritically repeating and even furthering the degrading and demeaning portrayal of non-white people and their culture found in *Heart of Darkness*: "Desai ends up linking Indian culture and Indian people with mad violence, historyless primitivism, gross animality, and even imputing to Hinduism the celebration of cannibalistic rites. In short, Desai has, I believe, in effect transformed the general population of India, especially Hindu India, into the semihuman savages of Conrad's Africa, in the most colonialist interpretation of that work" (36). However, in charging Desai with complicity in the perpetuation of colonial ideas and values, both Hogan and da Silva seem to me to ignore or take insufficient account of the fact that the blatant stereotyping of Indians and their culture goes on in passages that are either narrated by or focalized through European characters, and that their views are challenged rather than simply affirmed within the text itself. We have already established that Baumgartner's perspective, through which most of the narrative is filtered, is exposed as flawed and limited. The novel shows how his failure to understand Partition results from his failure to differentiate between Indians, his tendency to see them as a homogeneous mass. Hence, far from being immune to camp-thinking, he turns out to be guilty of the same offence that leads the Nazis, the British, and the Indians to exclude him. If Baumgartner's credibility is called into question, this is a fortiori the case for Kurt. To begin with, Kurt is a heroin addict, and it is strongly suggested that while making his speech about his experience of India he is high on drugs: Baumgartner finds "syringes and phials" afterwards in the bathroom of his apartment which Kurt had used (214). Moreover, Kurt's version of events is contradicted by the facts as presented in the novel. For example, his account of the flagellation, of walking in a procession and whipping himself ("he cut and lashed his body till the blood ran" [159]), is cast into doubt by the fact that he has no scars. Asked by Baumgartner where these are, he gives the following absurd answer: "I make myself whole again and again" (159). What is more, Kurt's speech culminates in an account of how he had "met and grappled with a yeti" (160)—which is, of course, a creature of legend, not of reality. The coda of his speech thus further undermines the junkie's credibility, as does the fact that Baumgartner himself questions the veracity of his stories: at one point, he interrupts Kurt, saying, "It is all dreams, my friend, mad dreams" (158).

To claim that *Baumgartner's Bombay* promotes orientalist stereotypes is thus to misinterpret the novel. Rather than a purveyor of colonial ideology, it seems to me, it is a study in cross-cultural incomprehension which parodies different forms of camp-thinking instead of uncritically reproducing them. The novel seeks to carve out a space "between camps" rather than within them, and calls upon the reader to transcend the racial and other divisions of camp-thinking. Exploring the complex interrelations between European and Asian traumatic histories, *Baumgartner's Bombay* suggests the need for a productive and dynamic cross-culturalism which could help break what it portrays as a global cycle of violence.

Conclusion

In this book, I have tried to expose the limitations and blind spots that I think trauma theory will need to confront if it is to deliver on its promise of cross-cultural ethical engagement. To some extent, this is already happening. Though in the early stages of its development trauma theory focused predominantly on the Holocaust, in recent years the field has begun to diversify. It now also includes a still relatively small but significant amount of work addressing other kinds of traumatic experiences, such as those associated with not only 9/11 but also slavery, colonialism, apartheid, Partition, and the Stolen Generations. Moreover, there is a growing number of publications that adopt a cross-cultural comparative perspective.[1] No doubt, much work remains to be done, especially, I think, regarding the conceptual and aesthetic issues that I have identified. However, these are hopeful signs, at least, that trauma theory is not irredeemably tainted with Eurocentric bias but can indeed stay relevant in the globalized world of the twenty-first century.

This relevance, however, cannot and should not be taken for granted. The ubiquity of trauma in contemporary United States culture has led to a number of trenchant and powerful critiques of—or even a backlash against—the recent interest in trauma, most notably by Mark Seltzer, Lauren Berlant, and Wendy Brown. Seltzer has famously identified a "wound culture" operating in society today: "the public fascination with torn and opened bodies and torn and opened persons, a collective gathering around shock, trauma, and the wound" (3). He characterizes the public sphere that is defined by this wound culture as a "pathological public sphere," that is, one

124

in which "the very notion of sociality is bound to the excitations of the torn and opened body, the torn and exposed individual, as public spectacle" (3–4). According to Seltzer, this pathological public sphere is inhabited by individuals who indulge in a voyeuristic fetishism of the other's wounds. Witnessing the suffering of others is not conducive to any kind of progressive social or political change, in his view—quite the contrary even: the cultural fixation on spectacles of suffering and trauma (such as car crashes or serial killings) is all about individuals indulging in erotic pleasure, enjoying a sadistic identification with violence and a masochistic identification with exposed pain.

Berlant has also expressed serious misgivings about the proliferation of images of suffering in the public sphere and the sentimental political discourse that, despite the popular belief in its positive workings, effectively uses these images to silence and commodify the voices of the oppressed. According to Berlant, this discourse turns pain into an object of mourning and thereby represents the sufferers as dead—indeed, mourning figures here as "an act of aggression, of social deathmaking" (307). In so doing, sentimental political discourse domesticates the traumatic impact of suffering on privileged and complacent spectators who are complicit in the exploitative system that engenders this suffering. Even well-meaning, progressive attempts to give a voice to the oppressed can fall prey to sentimental politics, and obscure the structural nature of oppression and inequality, when they presume "the *self-evidence* and therefore the *objectivity* of painful feeling" (309). Berlant suggests that "the tactical use of trauma to describe the effects of social inequality so overidentifies the eradication of pain with the achievement of justice that it enables various confusions: for instance, the equation of pleasure with freedom or the sense that changes in feeling, even on a mass scale, amount to substantial social change" (310–11). Meanwhile, the "overwhelming structural violence" of the system remains unaddressed; indeed, the "transpersonal linkages and intimacies" fostered by sentimental politics can come to serve as "proleptic shields," "ethically uncontestable legitimating devices for sustaining the hegemonic field" (311).

Similar doubts about the political value and efficacy of focusing on trauma and testimony have been voiced by Brown, who argues that identity politics in contemporary liberal society is based on an investment in "wounded attachments" that undercuts its emancipatory goals. The pursuit of a radically democratic political project is hindered, in Brown's view, by the tendency of subordinate groups to assume a victim position to confirm and legitimate an identity for themselves. Putting pain at the heart of demands for political recognition severely limits the possibilities for political transformation: "all that such pain may long for—more than revenge—is the chance to be heard into a certain release, recognized into self-overcoming, incited into possibilities for triumphing over, and hence losing, itself" (74–75). According to Brown, an effective oppositional politics may sustain such a project but must not be overtaken by it: she insists on the need to "guard[] against abetting the steady slide of political into therapeutic discourse, even as we acknowledge the elements of suffering and healing we might be negotiating" (75).[2]

Cogent though these various critiques are in their own terms, it seems to me that they unduly homogenize and simplify different forms of interest in and inquiry into trauma. While it is true, of course, that trauma research does not in and of itself lead to political transformation, I would argue that a trauma theory revised along the lines I have suggested is not destined to serve as the handmaiden of the status quo or a mere academic alibi for the indulgence of voyeuristic inclinations. On the contrary, it can help identify and understand situations of exploitation and abuse, and act as an incentive for the kind of sustained and systemic critique of societal conditions called for by Berlant and Brown. In fact, the expanded model of trauma I have proposed, based on the work of Laura Brown, Frantz Fanon, and others, bears a close resemblance to the model of suffering that Berlant puts forward as an alternative to the (traditional) trauma model, which she finds inadequate: "a model of *suffering*, whose etymological articulation of pain and patience draws its subject less as an effect of an act of violence and more as an effect of a general ntmosphere of it, peppered by acts, to be sure, but not contained by the presumption that trauma carries, that it is an effect of a single scene of violence or toxic taxonomy" (338). Berlant's observation that "the pain and suffering of subordinated subjects in everyday life is an ordinary and ongoing thing that is underdescribed by the (traumatic) identity form and its circulation in the state and the law" (344) is perfectly in line with the argument I have presented in this book.

That trauma research can act as a catalyst for astute political analysis and meaningful activism would seem to be borne out by the development in Fanon's writing, from *Black Skin, White Masks*, which describes the psychological impact of racial and colonial oppression, to the overtly political *The Wretched of the Earth*, which confronts the source of the mental strife he saw in the clinic.[3] Since Douglas Crimp's plea for "[m]ilitancy, of course, then, but mourning too: mourning *and* militancy" (18) in relation to the AIDS movement back in 1989, several scholars have argued that an interest in issues of trauma, loss, and mourning is in fact compatible with a commitment to radical activism. A desire to make visible the creative and political—rather than pathological and negative—aspects of an attachment to loss is the thread that binds together the essays gathered in David Eng and David Kazanjian's volume *Loss: The Politics of Mourning* (2003), which seeks to "extend[] recent scholarship in trauma studies by insisting that ruptures of experience, witnessing, history, and truth are, indeed, a starting point for political activism and transformation" (10). Eng and Kazanjian see their collection as moving "from trauma to prophecy, and from epistemological structures of unknowability to the politics of mourning" (10). As one of the contributors, Ann Cvetkovich, puts it, trauma can be "the provocation to create alternative lifeworlds" ("Legacies of Trauma" 453).[4]

Recognition of suffering serves as a necessary first step towards the amelioration of that suffering. In Judith Butler's words, "The recognition of shared precariousness introduces strong normative commitments of equality and invites a more robust universalizing of rights that seeks to address basic human needs for food, shelter, and other conditions for persisting and flourishing" (28–29). Without wishing to overstate its likely impact, I believe that rethinking trauma studies from a postcolonial perspective and providing nuanced readings of a wide variety of narratives of trauma and witnessing from around the world can help us understand that shared precariousness. By fostering attunement to previously unheard suffering and putting into global circulation memories of a broad range of traumatic histories, an inclusive and culturally sensitive trauma theory can assist in raising awareness of injustice both past and present and opening up the possibility of a more just global future—and, in so doing, remain faithful to the ethical foundations of the field.[5]

Notes

1 The Trauma of Empire

1. LaCapra has published two more monographs since then—*History in Transit: Experience, Identity, Critical Theory* (2004) and *History and Its Limits: Human, Animal, Violence* (2009)—but, unlike the aforementioned three books, neither of these are devoted to issues of trauma, at least not in their entirety: they each contain a single chapter on trauma studies in which LaCapra restates his views and answers his critics.

2. Later on in the book, Hartman reiterates this point, using italics for emphasis: "*It is my view that the failure to carry this imagination* [the trustworthy rural imagination in which Wordsworth placed his faith] *into a modern form, the failure to translate into a modern idiom a sensibility nurtured by country life, creates—less in England, because of Wordsworth, than in continental Europe—an unprogressive, overidealized, image of what is lost, and thus a deeply anti-urban sentiment.* . . . It is on the continent . . . that pastoralism eventually distorts cultural thinking and leads to serious political consequences" (73). A footnote to this passage makes it clear that Hartman is indeed referring to "the rise of fascism," a movement that "gained its strongest hold in places where industrialization threatened the greatest loss of the past or where preindustrial tradition resisted modernization" (92n.21). In his view, "the very absence on the continent of a Wordsworth or a Wordsworth reception removed what might have moderated a cultural and political antimodernism vulnerable to vicious dichotomies" (79).

3. According to Novak, the story of Tancred and Clorinda "reveals . . . that the discourse of trauma is founded upon an erasure of the voice of the Colonial Other" (32). Perceptive though Novak's analysis is, strictly speaking, Clorinda cannot be considered a *colonial* other: after all, Ethiopia is unique among African nations in that it has never been colonized by a European power (though it was briefly occupied by Italy from 1936 to 1941), and the era of the crusades during which *Gerusalemme Liberata* is set predates the colonial period in Africa by several centuries anyway, as does the time of the epic's composition

4. I am reminded here of Philip Gourevitch and Errol Morris's insistence that the story of Abu Ghraib, like the larger story of the Iraq war, was an American story, and that Iraq only happened to be the stage on which it was played out. In *Standard Operating Procedure: A War Story* (2008), their book about the 2004 Abu Ghraib torture and prisoner abuse scandal based on the eponymous documentary film directed by Morris, they argue that:

> The stain is ours, because whatever else the Iraq war was about, it was always, above all, about America—about the projection of America's

force and America's image into the world. Iraq was the stage, and Iraqis would suffer for that, enduring some fifty deaths for every American life lost: in this, and by every other measure of devastation, it was very much their war. But... the war was not their choice. It was an American war because America's elected officials decided to wage it of their own initiative, "at a time of our choosing," as the president said, and it was a war about America because it was fought in the name of our freedom and the world's. What was at stake, for the war's advocates, skeptics, and opponents alike, was an American story—the story of America as a champion of law and liberty at home and abroad, a tough but righteous arbiter of the destiny of nations, intolerant only of intolerance, a scourge to rogue regimes and bandit dictators who usurp the innate craving of all humankind to aspire to her example. (160)

Elaborating on this passage in response to criticism the book had received for telling the story exclusively through American eyes and voices—most notably those of soldiers involved in the abuses—and omitting the voices (and even the real names) of the Iraqi detainees who appear in the Abu Ghraib photographs, Gourevitch wrote: "To put it bluntly, the story of Abu Ghraib was not that Iraqi prisoners were being brutally abused—that was the norm in Iraq. The story was that Americans were doing the abusing—and that they were doing it as a matter of policy." He went on to argue that the victims' passivity made their stories less interesting than those of the perpetrators: "It is also far more powerful and more convincing and more damning to hear those people who are agents of violence describe the harm they did to their victims than to hear the victims describe it. A pure victim has no agency in his predicament; he makes no significant moral choices; he does not act, he is acted upon. That's why I never felt that the Iraqi voices were missing..." In a reply to Gourevitch's post (which appeared as part of a TPMCafe Book Club discussion about *Standard Operating Procedure*), a commenter by the name of Dan K called Gourevitch's claims "parochial" and "startlingly self-absorbed." He continued:

Confession and expiation can be just as self-absorbed as the crimes that give rise to these acts of contrition. "See our stain!" you seem to say. "See the beauty of our guilt! See the redeeming eloquence of our account of our transgressions! See how willingly and magnificently we drive the nails through our own wrists and ankles! We are guilty, guilty, guilty... and yet, we are nobly guilty, so admirably and articulately and awe-inspiringly conscious of our guilt, are we not? How could the repulsively passive and banal sufferings of our beastly victims—those film extras of life, with their annoying and inconvenient *names* and *identities*—possibly measure up to the drama of our confession and reckoning! They exist only as the necessary human props for the spectacle of our atonement. Whether we do great good or great evil, the story must remain *our* story."

In another comment on Gourevitch's post, Nick Flynn, himself the author of a book about the Abu Ghraib scandal, suggested that Morris's decision not to interview the Iraqi detainees—to whom, according to Flynn,

he did have access—"points to one of the reasons that Abu Ghraib happened, that is, the ways we are able to make 'the other' invisible." K's
and Flynn's criticisms of Gourevitch and Morris's approach to Abu Ghraib
obviously resonate with my own concerns about Caruth's treatment of the
non-European other in her work.

5. Given the amount of attention trauma theory has lavished on the experience of victimization, I find it rather striking, though, that one of
Caruth's key examples of trauma turns out to be an instance of perpetrator
trauma, a fact she does not readily acknowledge. As LaCapra writes, "One
might observe that her focus on the survivor-victim (indeed, the apparently ambiguous status of Tancred as perpetrator-victim who is termed in
passing a survivor) does not explicitly open itself to the formulation of
the specific problem of perpetrator trauma which her example seems to
foreground..." (*Writing History* 182). The example discussed in the next
paragraph—the trauma of the Hebrew people caused by their own murder of Moses—is another case in point of how an instance of perpetrator
trauma comes to stand in for trauma in general.

6. LaCapra makes the same point in *History and Memory after Auschwitz* (41),
History and Its Limits: Human, Animal, Violence (79), and *Writing History,
Writing Trauma*. To quote the latter:

> "Victim" is not a psychological category. It is, in variable ways, a social,
> political, and ethical category. Victims of certain events will in all like-
> lihood be traumatized by them, and not being traumatized would itself
> call for explanation. But not everyone traumatized by events is a vic-
> tim. There is the possibility of perpetrator trauma which must itself be
> acknowledged and in some sense worked through if perpetrators are
> to distance themselves from an earlier implication in deadly ideologies
> and practices. Such trauma does not, however, entail the equation or
> identification of the perpetrator and the victim. (79)

7. The mechanism we see at work here can be described in terms of
what LaCapra calls "vicarious victimhood" (*Writing History* 47), a process
whereby "the oppressors take over the position of the oppressed by shifting
the focus of empathetic identification back onto themselves" (Burrows 18).
As a result, the distress of the victim is appropriated, and the distinction
between aggressor and victim is obscured.

8. The first two quotations within this quotation are from Freud's *Moses and
Monotheism*, the others from Caruth's *Unclaimed Experience*. The additional
information enclosed in square brackets was inserted by Loye

9. In Caruth's defence, one might point to her inclusion in *Trauma: Explorations in Memory* of an essay by Georges Bataille, titled "Concerning the
Accounts Given by the Residents of Hiroshima," which focuses precisely
on the story that remains untold in *Hiroshima mon amour*. Moreover, Marie
Claire Ropars-Wuilleumier claims that, far from eclipsing the horror of
Hiroshima, the narration of the French woman's story serves to drive home
the devastating impact of a mass catastrophe that exceeds the limits of representation and is beyond mourning. This is how Nancy Wood summarizes
Ropars-Wuilleumier's argument:

she insists that we should not see this "psychoanalytic simulacrum" [the fact that the Japanese lover assumes the position of the analyst in the psychoanalytic encounter in relation to the French actress] as operating primarily on behalf of the "working-through" of the traumatic memory of *une femme tondue*. Rather, the elaboration of the Nevers story in this transferential mode implicitly poses the question of what it means to "work through" the legacy of an atomic catastrophe (or indeed any mass catastrophe), what comparable labour of mourning can release survivors—and societies—from the "psychic numbing" that the devastation induced as the very condition of survival? The "simple story" of Nevers is thus designated to assume the enormous affective weight of "the opaque memory of an event whose importance cannot be formulated." (187–89)

2 The Empire of Trauma

1. Michael Wessells has similarly warned against the use of psychology as "an instrument of cultural imperialism": "When this occurs, well intentioned intervention efforts inflict psychological damage through the continuation of historic patterns of oppression and external domination. In addition, there may be an erosion of local cultural beliefs and practices that are key resources for healing, and communities may be increasingly cut off from the traditions in which their sense of meaning and identity are grounded. As communities lose their voice, they slide further into passivity and silently give up hope in their own ability" (276). See also Bracken and Petty, eds.

2. An essay adapted from the book, titled "The Americanization of Mental Illness," appeared in the *New York Times Magazine* on 8 January 2010.

3. As Laura Brown observes, the DSM's list of illnesses found only in other cultures—such as *ataque de nervios*, *amok*, and *koro*—is "replete with posttraumatic responses framed in culturally specific manners" (*Cultural Competence* 8). See also L. Brown, *Cultural Competence* 163.

4. In a recent article in the *Boston Globe* titled "Do Some Cultures Have Their Own Ways of Going Mad?" Latif Nasser writes that, partly in response to criticism from a number of psychiatrists, anthropologists, and historians, "the DSM's editorial task force has convened a special committee of 20 advisers to figure out what to do with the category [of culture-bound syndromes]." While the inclusion of these illnesses in the DSM used to be perceived as "a triumph for the forces of inclusivity," the category now looks like "a ghetto—or, as critics have called it, a 'museum of exotica.' " The committee's recommendations for how the DSM-5 should handle culture-bound syndromes are currently being drafted, and may or may not be followed by the editors. According to Nasser, who interviewed the committee chair, Roberto Lewis-Fernández, "They [Lewis-Fernández and his team] suggest that a shorter appendix remain, winnowed down to a handful of well-documented problems. They'd also like a stronger statement about culture's role in mental illness in the introduction, and the

disorders mentioned in the DSM itself." However, what is apparently not on the table yet is "a deeper acknowledgment that far more mental illnesses might be cultural than we currently think." Including typically Western syndromes—Nasser cites chronic fatigue syndrome and multiple personality disorder—in the culture-bound category would be "politically unfeasible," Lewis-Fernández is quoted as saying. However, "for many in the global psychiatry community," Nasser concludes, "that argument is already over: It's time for Westerners to realize that their mental illnesses might be, one way or another, just as much a local product as pibloktoq [one of the acknowledged culture-bound syndromes]."

5. It can be argued, however, that such incidents are "the almost daily reminders of the threat of violence that underlies bias" (L. Brown, *Cultural Competence* 103).

6. Bergner shows how psychoanalysis can work to suppress racial trauma in an insightful analysis of the 1949 Hollywood film *Home of the Brave*, directed by Mark Robson: "It is a story about a black soldier during World War II who suffers a sort of shell shock and must be cured through psychoanalytic therapy. In the course of the therapy, the psychoanalyst 'discovers' that the soldier's symptoms stem from a racial inferiority complex rather than the horrors of war. The doctor attempts to 'cure' the soldier of *his* race complex, thereby locating the problem of American racism in the African-American subject" (226). While the film "gestures toward an acknowledgment of the psychologically debilitating effects of material and ideological discrimination," Bergner writes, it "winds up mainly pathologizing the victim" (231).

7. As Rebecca Saunders and Kamran Aghaie observe, "It is easier—and cheaper—to pathologize individuals than to critique or dismantle systems of war, empire, patriarchy, economic inequality, or racism" (19).

8. This risk also haunts Summerfield's own discourse: after all, the phrase *the non-Western mind* smacks of racial essentialism.

9. On Fanon as a trauma theorist, see also Kaplan, "Fanon, Trauma and Cinema"; Kennedy; and Saunders and Aghaie. Given its numerous valuable insights, which I go on to outline below, it is remarkable that Fanon's work is altogether absent from most histories of the concept of trauma, including the accounts of Herman, Allan Young, Ruth Leys, Roger Luckhurst, and Didier Fassin and Richard Rechtman—a state of affairs that reflects the traditional neglect of race in trauma research. Directing her critical attention to Leys, Burrows denounces "the limited focus" of the former's book *Trauma: A Genealogy* (2000), which Burrows describes as "a text that is premised entirely upon a Eurocentric reading solely indentured to a middle-class whiteness built on concepts of Western individualism" (17). As Burrows points out, Leys's book fails to live up to its promise of a comprehensive analysis of the history of the conceptualization of trauma as it lacks "a substantial exploration of racism," despite this being a major source of trauma in the twentieth and—Burrows predicts— twenty-first centuries (17). Burrows therefore calls for "a comprehensive

remapping of trauma theory that is not white-centric and gender-blind" (17).

10. According to E. Ann Kaplan, Fanon's experience, which she analyses in some detail, "can now be defined as a fairly classic trauma" ("Fanon, Trauma and Cinema" 147). While I agree with the "trauma" part of this formulation, the traumatic stressor strikes me as anything but "fairly classic" in this case, as it falls outside the DSM definition.

11. The fact that LaCapra frames the problem facing post-apartheid South Africa as one of "acknowledging and working through historical losses" (*Writing History* 44) would seem to suggest that he does understand racism as a historical trauma.

12. For another discussion of LaCapra's distinction between historical and structural trauma in relation to race, see Burrows 18–19.

13. In fact, Wilder proposes a modified concept of working-through that could adequately address the trauma of racism as a supplement to the psychoanalytic version that corresponds to historical trauma: "A modified concept of working through would no longer mean transcending a pathology by attempting to master or resolve it, but acting in terms of (by moving through rather than over or around) the unavoidable socio-epistemological framework provided by a durable and persistent legacy in order to move beyond it" (55). Another promising attempt to develop new concepts responsive to the traumas associated with racial and colonial oppression is Jacques Derrida's theorization of "mid-mourning," which refuses the traditional distinction between mourning and melancholia, and which I will come back to in Chapter 5. Sam Durrant draws on Derrida's work in *Postcolonial Narrative and the Work of Mourning* (2004) to articulate a postcolonial ethics of inconsolable mourning that recognizes the impossibility of retrieving or recovering the past. Interestingly, LaCapra has criticized Durrant's variant of trauma theory for "collaps[ing] the distinction between melancholy and mourning" (*History and Its Limits* 61n.3). Also highly relevant, it seems to me, is Seth Moglen's revision of the Freudian model of melancholia and mourning, which aims to turn these concepts into useful tools for describing the processes by which individuals and groups manage experiences of social injury such as racism, misogyny, homophobia, and economic exploitation. Moglen proposes a triadic model of mourning, which allows the anger felt by the mourner to be directed not only at him- or herself or at the lost object, as in the traditional dyadic model, but also at the social forces that have produced a particular experience of collective loss.

14. Derrida's essay "Geopsychoanalysis: '...and the rest of the world,'" which comments on the blindness of psychoanalysis to most of the world, is included in Christopher Lane's collection *The Psychoanalysis of Race* and is also invoked by Ranjana Khanna (1–2).

15. For two recent overviews of and contributions to the debate about the relationship between poststructuralism and deconstruction on the one hand and the postcolonial on the other, see Syrotinski and Hiddleston.

16. An earlier version of the relevant Chapter 28 from *Postcolonialism: An Historical Introduction*, titled "Subjectivity and History: Derrida in Algeria," was published as "Deconstruction and the Postcolonial" in Nicholas Royle's edited collection *Deconstructions: A User's Guide* (2000).

17. For example, Terry Eagleton locates the roots of poststructuralism in the aftermath of the events of May 1968 in *Literary Theory: An Introduction* (1996) to explain its alleged withdrawal from history and politics: "Post-structuralism was a product of that blend of euphoria and disillusionment, liberation and dissipation, carnival and catastrophe, which was 1968. Unable to break the structures of state power, post-structuralism found it possible instead to subvert the structures of language. Nobody, at least, was likely to beat you over the head for doing so" (122).

3   Beyond Trauma Aesthetics

1. As Felski points out, efforts to develop such an aesthetic are "reminiscent of similar unresolved debates in the domain of Marxist aesthetics" (1).

2. As Rothberg points out, this claim is debatable: "one is justified in asking why it [Beckett's art] too cannot be appropriated by the culture industry"— which "is precisely what happens, according to [Fredric] Jameson, during the transition to postmodernism" (*Traumatic Realism* 41).

3. LaCapra voices his suspicion of empathy "when autonomized or made to function as a substitute (rather than a motivation) for social and political action, notably with respect to victims": "Empathy is at best one component of a larger constellation of forces or factors in both historical understanding and sociopolitical action, and it must be approached situationally and in terms of its differential deployment" (*History and Its Limits* 67n.14). Denouncing the tendency to see empathy as a self-sufficient response, LaCapra argues that empathy "must be articulated with . . . normative judgment and sociopolitical response" (*History in Transit* 135). He maintains that cultural and political critique, if they are to be meaningful, must be informed by empathy: "there can be no durable ethical and political change without the reeducation of affect in its relation to normative judgment" (*History in Transit* 137).

4   Ordinary Trauma in Sindiwe Magona's *Mother to Mother*

1. This acknowledgement, and the motivation behind it, can be found in the *TRC Report*, vol. 1, ch. 4.

2. That the debate about the merits of the psychotherapeutic framework adopted by the TRC is still far from settled became clear at a University of Cape Town conference marking the tenth anniversary of the start of the TRC in November 2006. See the ensuing polemic between Kay Schaffer and Jaco Barnard in *Borderlands E-Journal*, which revolved around the question

of whether a psychotherapeutic approach to healing and reconciliation is compatible with political commitment.

3. Samuelson goes on to observe, as I do here, that Magona "render[s] visible the 'ordinary' structural violence underpinning the 'spectacular' event of Biehl's death" (*Remembering* 167).

4. In fact, the *TRC Report* itself gently rebuffs the temporal limits placed on the commission's mandate. It opens, after the chairman's foreword, with a chapter on history, which states that the period from 1960 to 1994 was only "the climactic phase of a conflict that dated back to the mid-seventeenth century, to the time when European settlers first sought to establish a permanent presence on the subcontinent" (vol. 1, ch. 2, par. 5). It points out that the National Party government did not "introduce[] racially discriminatory practices to this part of the world" and is unlikely to have been "the first to perpetrate some or most of the types of gross violations of human rights recorded in this report" (vol. 1, ch. 2, par. 6). Indeed, the atrocities committed during the period falling within the TRC's mandate have to be put in the context of previous violations (vol. 1, ch. 2, par. 7). "It is also important to remember," the report goes on, "that the 1960 Sharpville massacre (with which the mandate of the Commission begins) was simply the latest in a long line of similar killings of civilian protesters in South African history" (vol. 1, ch. 2, par. 8). Moreover, it maintains that the social-engineering dimension of the policy of apartheid did not mark a radical break with the past either: "Again, it needs to be made clear that the National Party was not the first political party or group to have been accused of social engineering on a vast scale in this part of the world" (vol. 1, ch. 2, par. 10).

5. On the numerous religious references in *Mother to Mother*, see also Samuelson, "The Mother as Witness" 135–36.

6. The novel's reliance on storm imagery, which naturalizes racial conflict as a normal and unavoidable state of affairs, may seem to suggest otherwise, though.

7. Magona's novel also resonates powerfully with a remarkable true story of forgiveness and friendship between two mothers featured on *TED* in May 2011: the American Phyllis Rodriguez, whose son died in the World Trade Center attacks on 11 September 2001, and Aicha el-Wafi, a Moroccan-born French woman whose son Zacarias Moussaoui—the alleged "twentieth hijacker"—was convicted of a role in those attacks and is serving a life sentence without parole.

5   Mid-Mourning in David Dabydeen's "Turner" and Fred D'Aguiar's *Feeding the Ghosts*

1. The experience of the Middle Passage has been interpreted as a founding trauma for people of African descent by Edouard Glissant and Paul Gilroy, much of whose work is dedicated to excavating the long shadow of the Middle Passage in contemporary Caribbean and black Atlantic culture. See Glissant's *Caribbean Discourse: Selected Essays* (1989) and *Poetics*

of Relation (1997 [1990]), and Gilroy's *The Black Atlantic: Modernity and Double Consciousness* (1993).

2. To be precise, ten of these 132 slaves threw themselves overboard in a display of defiance against the inhumanity of the proceedings. The *Zong* massacre also features in Michelle Cliff's novels *Abeng* (1984) and *Free Enterprise* (2004), Dabydeen's novel *A Harlot's Progress* (1999), M. NourbeSe Philip's poetry collection *Zong!* (2008), and Marina Warner's novel *Indigo* (1992), a further testimony to the centrality that this event has assumed in the contemporary literary imagination of the slave past.

3. A similar argument can be made in relation to Toni Morrison's celebrated novel *Beloved* (1987), which is haunted by the memory of slavery, including the Middle Passage, to which it makes frequent reference. See Durrant 79–109 for a particularly insightful analysis of *Beloved* and its (mid-)mourning work.

4. For a detailed analysis of Dabydeen's poetic reaction to Turner's painting and its reception, see Ward 97–112.

5. The echo from Fanon has been noted in passing by Erik Falk (191). However, Falk's reading of "Turner," which sings the praises of creative amnesia—"the loss of memory, history and identity … constitutes a history that must, ultimately, be 'forgotten' for a new and unpredictable future to be possible" (188)—seems to me to assimilate the poem to an apocalyptic discourse which, as I argue here, it critiques rather than affirms.

6. This is just one of many ways in which symbolic and physical violence are connected in the poem. The most obvious example of such intermingling is Dabydeen's decision to call the slave-ship captain "Turner," which suggests a direct link between the artist's pictorial representation of slaves and the captain's sadistic abuse of the slave children under his care (see also Dabydeen, Preface 8). In fact, the poem exposes both Turner's painting and the "fable" (I. 22) which the speaker sets out to tell as harmful forms of denial. If, as Tobias Döring argues, the poem engages in "a critique of the cultural commodifications by which the terrors of the [slave] trade have become transfigured as aesthetic objects produced for the delectation of spectators and perceived as icons within English identity construction" (39), the speaker's own attempts at transfiguration are not exempt from this critique.

7. Dabydeen himself has described "Turner" as "a great howl of pessimism about the inability to recover anything meaningful from the past" (qtd in Dawes 200)—an interpretation which, to my mind, takes too negative a view of negativity.

8. Louise Yelin also ascribes liberating potential to the poem's "rhetoric of negation": in "remember[ing] his own history as negation," she argues, the speaker "negotiates a provisional escape route from the bondage of Turner's economy of representation" (362).

9. "Unhomely" is a literal translation of Freud's term *Unheimliche*, which is commonly translated as "uncanny." *Das Unheimliche* refers to a peculiar kind of anxiety resulting from the return of a familiar phenomenon

made strange by repression (Freud, "The Uncanny")—in this context, the history of the Middle Passage embodied by Mintah's discomforting sculptures, which the (about-to-be-ex-)slave community has repressed, banished from the domestic sphere of the home.

10. As Ward points out, "The intention is for the past to be 'laid to rest' when told, but the novel proves this to be an unrealistic aim: once again, the problems of remembering slavery come to preoccupy the novel" (159).

6 Cross-Traumatic Affiliation

1. For an account of the impact of *Holocaust* in Germany, see Huyssen, "The Politics of Identification: 'Holocaust' and West German Drama."

2. See also the nuanced account of memory and globalization offered by Andreas Huyssen in *Present Pasts: Urban Palimpsests and the Politics of Memory* (2003).

3. Originally titled "On the Social Construction of Moral Universals: The 'Holocaust' from War Crime to Trauma Drama," the essay was reprinted, together with a number of critical responses to it, in Alexander et al.'s *Remembering the Holocaust: A Debate* (2009).

4. For incisive critiques of Levy and Sznaider's and Alexander's arguments, see A. Assmann; Moses, "Genocide and the Terror of History"; Poole; and the various responses to Alexander's essay included in Alexander et al.'s *Remembering the Holocaust*.

5. See, for example, Jay; Manne; and Moses, "Genocide and the Terror of History." In the postscript to *Remembering the Holocaust*, as well as in a more recent essay co-authored with Shai Dromi, Alexander concedes that the case of Israel shows how the trauma drama of the Holocaust can become a recipe for conflict without end. The latter essay, which originally appeared in 2011, is included in Alexander's newly published book *Trauma: A Social Theory* (2012), which also reprints "On the Social Construction of Moral Universals: The 'Holocaust' from War Crime to Trauma Drama."

6. *Iraq Body Count*, a web-based effort to record civilian deaths resulting from the US-led 2003 invasion of Iraq, puts the number of Iraqi civilians killed in the war and occupation between 105,177 and 114,874.

7. The idea that, in the United States, Holocaust memory acts as a convenient distraction from the blackest pages of the nation's own history can also be found in the work of Edward Linenthal, Peter Novick, Lilian Friedberg, and Ward Churchill, among others. See Rothberg, *Multidirectional Memory* 12–16 and Neil Levi for useful overviews and discussions of the Holocaust-as-screen-memory debate.

8. Charles Maier distinguishes between two moral-atrocity narratives for the twentieth century: a Western one that sees the Holocaust and/or Stalinist oppression as the pre-eminent historical experience of the century, and one that comes from "the rest of the world" and centres on the domination of the West over the global South in the form of imperialism and neo-colonialism.

9. Rothberg similarly notes that "the use of the Holocaust as a metaphor or analogy for other events and histories has emerged precisely because the Holocaust is widely thought of as a unique and uniquely terrible form of political violence. Assertions of uniqueness thus actually produce further metaphorical and analogical appropriations (which, in turn, prompt further assertions of uniqueness)" (*Multidirectional Memory* 11).

10. For a collection that deals specifically with this oft-neglected dimension of Arendt's political theory, see King and Stone, eds.

11. Rothberg devotes three insightful chapters to Arendt's, Césaire's, and Du Bois's work in *Multidirectional Memory*. He argues that Du Bois arrived at a more nuanced understanding of the relation between the Nazi genocide and colonial violence in his 1949 article "The Negro and the Warsaw Ghetto," where he no longer interprets the former as a simple repeat of the latter but recognizes the differences as well as the similarities between them (*Multidirectional Memory* 124).

12. Cheyette discusses Phillips's *The Nature of Blood* and Desai's *Baumgartner's Bombay* together in an essay that focuses specifically on the novels' representation of Venice, a city that plays a prominent role in both texts ("Venetian Spaces").

7 Jewish/Postcolonial Diasporas in the Work of Caryl Phillips

1. According to Walkowitz, "Phillips's novels, anthologies, and essays offer compelling examples of the new world literature and of what I call 'comparison literature,' an emerging genre of world literature for which global comparison is a formal as well as a thematic preoccupation" ("Location" 536).

2. This is also the case, though less obviously, in his novels *Crossing the River* (1993) and *A Distant Shore* (2003), as well as in his travel book *The Atlantic Sound* (2000). Gordon Collier has argued that Joyce, one of the main characters in *Crossing the River*, might be Jewish, though he admits that this is "unprovable" as "almost all of the traces have been scuffled over" (195). Even so, he makes a fairly strong case for regarding Joyce as "a revenant of Irene [from *Higher Ground*], an exemplar of the Jewish culture so often pondered in Phillips's essays, a precursor of Eva Stern [from *The Nature of Blood*]—and an echo of the Jew 'somewhere in [Phillips's] family' " (195). There is also a minor (presumably) Jewish character in *A Distant Shore*: Dr Epstein, who tried to establish herself in an English village but, according to the barman in the local pub, did not "blend in" (9). Finally, references to Jewish history and anti-Semitism can be found throughout *The Atlantic Sound*.

3. In the same essay, Phillips mentions how, "as a black man living in Europe," he always remembers the words of Frantz Fanon, who in 1952 wrote of his philosophy professor, a native of the Antilles, warning him: "Whenever you hear anyone abuse the Jews, pay attention, because he is talking about you" (54).

4. See, for example, Mantel.
5. See also Dawson 95–96, Thomas 57, and Whitehead 102. Zierler, by contrast, reads Othello's visit to the ghetto as an example of "Jews and blacks recogniz[ing] themselves in each other" (64). Another overly affirmative reading of this episode is offered by Helge Nowak, who claims that "Caryl Phillips is at pains to establish a bond of mutual sympathy between the Moor and the Jews of Venice in the narration of Othello's visits to the ghetto and of his meeting with a Jewish scholar" (131).
6. Other intertexts include famous literary and testimonial accounts of the Holocaust by Primo Levi, Cynthia Ozick, André Schwarz-Bart, and Elie Wiesel.

8   Entangled Memories in Anita Desai's *Baumgartner's Bombay*

1. As she explains to Feroza Jussawalla and Lalita Pandit, Desai could not find any official records of the British internment camps in India. However, her mother had known several former inmates, who had talked to them about their imprisonment, so Desai was aware of their existence. Moreover, once she had completed the chapter in question she had it checked by several people familiar with the camps, including a Jewish professor in Israel who had been held there (Jussawalla 175; Pandit 170–71).
2. The first people to arrive on the murder scene after Kurt has fled finish the job for him. Baumgartner's cats are stuffed into sacks and taken away by rag-pickers, and Chimanlal's son orders the murdered man's body to be removed and the apartment to be cleared of its contents, so that it can be handed over to the landlord. Thus, within hours after his death Baumgartner has disappeared without a trace; his life is completely obliterated, just as the Nazis intended.
3. For a more extensive discussion of the role of Venice in *Baumgartner's Bombay* and *The Nature of Blood*, see Cheyette, "Venetian Spaces."
4. The parallel between European Jews and India's Muslim minority is the specific focus of Mufti's study *Enlightenment in the Colony: The Jewish Question and the Crisis of Postcolonial Culture* (2007).

Conclusion

1. See, for example, Michael Rothberg's *Multidirectional Memory: Remembering the Holocaust in the Age of Decolonization* (2009), Sophie Croisy's *Other Cultures of Trauma: Meta-Metropolitan Narratives and Identities* (2007), Victoria Burrows's *Whiteness and Trauma: The Mother-Daughter Knot in the Fiction of Jean Rhys, Jamaica Kincaid and Toni Morrison* (2004), Sam Durrant's *Postcolonial Narrative and the Work of Mourning* (2004), and several collections, such as *World Memory: Personal Trajectories in Global Time* (Bennett and Kennedy, eds.; 2003), *Trauma Texts* (Whitlock and Douglas, eds.; 2009),

The Splintered Glass: Facets of Trauma in the Post-Colony and Beyond (Herrero and Baelo-Allué, eds.; 2011), and special issues of *Comparative Studies of South Asia, Africa and the Middle East* (Saunders and Aghaie, eds.; 2005), *Studies in the Novel* (Craps and Buelens, eds.; 2008), *Continuum: Journal of Media and Cultural Studies* (Traverso and Broderick, eds.; 2010), *Yale French Studies* (Rothberg et al., eds.; 2010); and *Criticism: A Quarterly for Literature and the Arts* (Craps and Rothberg, eds.; 2011).

2. In the same vein, Berlant denounces "the therapeutic conversion of the scene of pain and its eradication to the scene of the political itself" (314). "The reparation of pain," she reminds us, "does not bring into being a just life" (337).

3. E. Ann Kaplan interprets Fanon's "revolutionary zeal" as "an unconscious effort to cancel out the trauma that marked him as a reviled object to the white child because of his black skin" ("Fanon, Trauma and Cinema" 154): it is this "psychic syndrome" that propelled him to focus on "institutional and social change" ("Fanon, Trauma and Cinema" 155). While I do not rule out the possibility that Fanon's unconscious may have played a role in determining the course of his work, I would hesitate to consign what strikes me as a profound insight into the inextricability of the discourses of trauma and politics to the realm of the unconscious, as Kaplan seems to be doing here.

4. See also Cvetkovich's monograph *An Archive of Feelings: Trauma, Sexuality, and Lesbian Public Cultures* (2003), in which she "explor[es] how trauma can be a foundation for creating counterpublic spheres rather than evacuating them" (15).

5. Even so, I accept Andreas Huyssen's caveat about the prevalence of the concern with trauma in memory studies: "to collapse memory into trauma, I think, would unduly confine our understanding of memory, marking it too exclusively in terms of pain, suffering, and loss" (*Present Pasts* 8). While I am not entirely convinced that an exclusive focus on trauma would necessarily "deny human agency and lock us into compulsive repetition" (*Present Pasts* 8), I do share Carrie Hamilton's concern that "trauma not be allowed to displace other theories and models of memory" lest "the positive legacies of past activisms" are left unexplored (276).

Bibliography

Abani, Christopher. *GraceLand*. New York: Farrar, 2004.

Achebe, Chinua. "An Image of Africa: Racism in Conrad's *Heart of Darkness*." *Hopes and Impediments: Selected Essays, 1965–1987*. By Achebe. London: Heinemann, 1988. 1–13.

Adichie, Chimamanda Ngozi. *Half of a Yellow Sun*. New York: Knopf, 2006.

Adorno, Theodor. "Commitment." 1962. Trans. Andrew Arato. *The Essential Frankfurt School Reader*. Ed. Andrew Arato and Elke Gebhardt. New York: Continuum, 1982. 300–18.

———. "Cultural Criticism and Society." 1951. *Prisms*. Trans. Samuel Weber and Shierry Weber. Cambridge: MIT, 1984. 17–34.

Ahmad, Aijaz. "The Politics of Literary Postcoloniality." *Race and Class* 36.3 (1995): 1–20.

Alexander, Jeffrey C. "On the Global and Local Representations of the Holocaust Tragedy." *Remembering the Holocaust: A Debate*. By Alexander et al. Oxford: Oxford UP, 2009. 173–92.

———. "On the Social Construction of Moral Universals: The 'Holocaust' from War Crime to Trauma Drama." *European Journal of Social Theory* 5.1 (2002): 5–85.

———. "The Social Construction of Moral Universals." *Remembering the Holocaust: A Debate*. By Alexander et al. Oxford: Oxford UP, 2009. 3–102.

———. *Trauma: A Social Theory*. Cambridge: Polity, 2012.

Alexander, Jeffrey C., and Shai Dromi. "Trauma Construction and Moral Restriction: The Ambiguity of the Holocaust for Israel." *Narrating Trauma: On the Impact of Collective Suffering*. Ed. Ron Eyerman, Jeffrey C. Alexander, and Elizabeth Butler Breese. Boulder: Paradigm, 2011. 107–32.

American Psychiatric Association. *Diagnostic and Statistical Manual of Mental Disorders*. 3rd ed. Washington: American Psychiatric Association, 1980.

———. *Diagnostic and Statistical Manual of Mental Disorders*. 3rd ed., rev. Washington: American Psychiatric Association, 1987.

———. *Diagnostic and Statistical Manual of Mental Disorders*. 4th ed. Washington: American Psychiatric Association, 1994.

———. *Diagnostic and Statistical Manual of Mental Disorders*. 4th ed., text rev. Washington: American Psychiatric Association, 2000.

———. "Rationale for Proposed Revision of Diagnostic Criteria for Posttraumatic Stress Disorder for DSM-5." *Proposed Draft Revisions to DSM Disorders and Criteria*. 10 Feb. 2010. 11 Mar. 2010. http://www.dsm5.org/ProposedRevisions/Pages/proposedrevision.aspx?rid=165.

Arendt, Hannah. *The Origins of Totalitarianism*. 1951. New York: Schocken, 2004.

Arruti, Nerea. "Trauma, Therapy, and Representation: Theory and Critical Reflection." *Paragraph: A Journal of Modern Critical Theory* 30.1 (2007): 1–8.

Assmann, Aleida. "The Holocaust—a Global Memory? Extensions and Limits of a New Memory Community." *Memory in a Global Age: Discourses, Practices and Trajectories.* Ed. Aleida Assmann and Sebastian Conrad. Houndmills: Palgrave Macmillan, 2010. 97–117.

Assmann, Aleida, and Sebastian Conrad. Introduction. *Memory in a Global Age: Discourses, Practices and Trajectories.* Ed. Aleida Assmann and Sebastian Conrad. Houndmills: Palgrave Macmillan, 2010. 1–16.

Assmann, Jan. *Das kulturelle Gedächtnis: Schrift, Erinnerung, und Identität in den frühen Hochkulturen.* München: C. H. Beck, 1992.

———. *Moses the Egyptian: The Memory of Egypt in Western Monotheism.* Cambridge: Harvard UP, 1997.

Ball, Karyn. "Trauma and Its Institutional Destinies." Introduction. *Trauma and Its Cultural Aftereffects.* Ed. Karyn Ball. Spec. issue of *Cultural Critique* 46 (Fall 2000): 1–44.

Barnard, Jaco. "Reflecting on Achievements, Celebrating Failures: A Response to Kay Schaffer." *Borderlands E-Journal* 6.1 (2007): n. pag. 23 Jan. 2008. http://www.borderlandsejournal.adelaide.edu.au/vol6no1_2007/barnard_reflecting.htm.

Bataille, Georges. "Concerning the Accounts Given by the Residents of Hiroshima." *Trauma: Explorations in Memory.* Ed. Cathy Caruth. Baltimore: Johns Hopkins UP, 1995. 221–35.

Baucom, Ian. "Specters of the Atlantic." *South Atlantic Quarterly* 100.1 (2001): 61–82.

Beah, Ishmael. *A Long Way Gone: Memoirs of a Boy Soldier.* London: Fourth Estate, 2007.

Bennett, Jill, and Rosanne Kennedy. Introduction. *World Memory: Personal Trajectories in Global Time.* Ed. Jill Bennett and Rosanne Kennedy. Houndmills: Palgrave Macmillan, 2003. 1–15.

———, eds. *World Memory: Personal Trajectories in Global Time.* Houndmills: Palgrave Macmillan, 2003.

Bergner, Gwen. "Politics and Pathologies: On the Subject of Race in Psychoanalysis." *Frantz Fanon: Critical Perspectives.* Ed. Anthony C. Alessandrini. London: Routledge, 1999. 219–34.

Berlant, Lauren. "The Subject of True Feeling: Pain, Privacy, and Politics." *Traumatizing Theory: The Cultural Politics of Affect in and beyond Psychoanalysis.* Ed. Karyn Ball. New York: Other, 2007. 305–47.

Bettelheim, Bruno. "The Ignored Lessons of Anne Frank." *Surviving and Other Essays.* By Bettelheim. London: Thames and Hudson, 1979. 246–57.

Bracken, Patrick J., and Celia Petty, eds. *Rethinking the Trauma of War.* London: Free Association, 1998.

Brink, André. "Stories of History: Reimagining the Past in Post-Apartheid Narrative." *Negotiating the Past: The Making of Memory in South Africa.* Ed. Sarah Nuttall and Carli Coetzee. Oxford: Oxford UP, 1998. 29–42.

Brown, Laura S. *Cultural Competence in Trauma Therapy: Beyond the Flashback.* Washington: American Psychological Association, 2008.

———. "Not Outside the Range: One Feminist Perspective on Psychic Trauma." *Trauma: Explorations in Memory*. Ed. Cathy Caruth. Baltimore: Johns Hopkins UP, 1995. 100–12.

Brown, Wendy. *States of Injury: Power and Freedom in Late Modernity*. Princeton: Princeton UP, 1995.

Bryant-Davis, Thema, and Carlota Ocampo. "Racist Incident-Based Trauma." *Counseling Psychologist* 33 (2005): 479–500.

Burrows, Victoria. *Whiteness and Trauma: The Mother-Daughter Knot in the Fiction of Jean Rhys, Jamaica Kincaid and Toni Morrison*. New York: Palgrave Macmillan, 2004.

Butler, Judith. *Frames of War: When Is Life Grievable?* London: Verso, 2009.

Caruth, Cathy. Preface. *Trauma: Explorations in Memory*. Ed. Cathy Caruth. Baltimore: Johns Hopkins UP, 1995. vii–ix.

———. "Trauma and Experience." Introduction. *Trauma: Explorations in Memory*. Ed. Cathy Caruth. Baltimore: Johns Hopkins UP, 1995. 3–12.

———. *Unclaimed Experience: Trauma, Narrative, and History*. Baltimore: Johns Hopkins UP, 1996.

Césaire, Aimé. *Discourse on Colonialism*. 1950. Trans. Joan Pinkham. New York: Monthly Review, 2000.

Cheyette, Bryan. "Jewish/Postcolonial Diasporas: On Being Ill-Disciplined." Introduction. *Jewish/Postcolonial Diasporas*. Ed. Cheyette. Spec. issue of *Wasafiri* 24.1 (2009): 1–2.

———. "Venetian Spaces: Old-New Literatures and the Ambivalent Uses of Jewish History." *Reading the "New" Literatures in a Postcolonial Era*. Ed. Susheila Nasta. Cambridge: Brewer, 2000. 53–72.

Chikane, Frank. "Children in Turmoil: The Effects of the Unrest on Township Children." *Growing Up in a Divided Society: The Contexts of Childhood in South Africa*. Ed. Sandra Burman and Pamela Reynolds. Johannesburg: Ravan, 1986. 333–44.

Churchill, Ward. *A Little Matter of Genocide: Holocaust and Denial in the Americas, 1492 to the Present*. San Francisco: City Lights, 1997.

Cliff, Michelle. *Abeng*. Trumansburg: Crossing, 1984.

———. *Free Enterprise*. San Francisco: City Lights, 2004.

Clingman, Stephen. "Forms of History and Identity in *The Nature of Blood*." *Salmagundi* 143 (2004): 141–66.

Coetzee, J. M. "What We Like to Forget." Rev. of *The Nature of Blood*, by Caryl Phillips. *New York Review of Books*. 6 Nov. 1997: 38–41.

Collier, Gordon. "Serene Surface, Secret Depths? Joyce's Section in *Crossing the River*." *Postcolonial Knitting: The Art of Jacqueline Bardolph*. Ed. Richard Corballis and André Viola. Palmerston North/Nice: Massey University/Université de Nice, 2000. 185–96.

Colvin, Christopher J. "'Brothers and Sisters, Do Not Be Afraid of Me': Trauma, History and the Therapeutic Imagination in the New South Africa." *Memory, History, Nation: Contested Pasts*. Ed. Katharine Hodgkin and Susannah Radstone. New Brunswick: Transaction, 2006. 153–67.

Conrad, Joseph. *Heart of Darkness*. 1902. New York: Norton, 2006.

Craps, Stef, and Gert Buelens, eds. *Postcolonial Trauma Novels*. Spec. issue of *Studies in the Novel* 40.1–2 (2008).

Craps, Stef, and Michael Rothberg, eds. *Transcultural Negotiations of Holocaust Memory*. Spec. issue of *Criticism: A Quarterly for Literature and the Arts* 53.4 (2011).

Crimp, Douglas. "Mourning and Militancy." *October* 51 (Winter 1989): 3–18.

Croisy, Sophie. *Other Cultures of Trauma: Meta-Metropolitan Narratives and Identities*. Saarbrücken: VDM Verlag Dr. Müller, 2007.

Cvetkovich, Ann. *An Archive of Feelings: Trauma, Sexuality, and Lesbian Public Cultures*. Durham: Duke UP, 2003.

———. "Legacies of Trauma, Legacies of Activism." *Loss: The Politics of Mourning*. Ed. David L. Eng and David Kazanjian. Berkeley: U of California P, 2003. 427–57.

Dabydeen, David. *A Harlot's Progress*. London: Jonathan Cape, 1999.

———. Preface. *Turner: New and Selected Poems*. By Dabydeen. 1995. Leeds: Peepal Tree, 2002. 7–8.

———. "Turner." *Turner: New and Selected Poems*. By Dabydeen. 1995. Leeds: Peepal Tree, 2002. 9–42.

D'Aguiar, Fred. *Feeding the Ghosts*. 1997. London: Vintage, 1998.

———. "The Last Essay about Slavery." *The Age of Anxiety*. Ed. Sarah Dunant and Roy Porter. London: Virago, 1996. 125–47.

———. *The Longest Memory*. London: Chatto and Windus, 1994.

da Silva, Tony Simoes. "Whose Bombay Is It Anyway? Anita Desai's *Baumgartner's Bombay*." *ARIEL: A Review of International English Literature* 28.3 (1997): 63–77. Literature Resource Center. Gale. Katholieke Universiteit Leuven. 12 Mar. 2009. http://go.galegroup.com/ps/start.do?p=LitRC&u=leuven.

Dawes, Kwame. "Interview with David Dabydeen." 1994. *The Art of David Dabydeen*. Ed. Kevin Grant. Leeds: Peepal Tree, 1997. 199–221.

Dawson, Ashley. "'To remember too much is indeed a form of madness': Caryl Phillips's *The Nature of Blood* and the Modalities of European Racism." *Postcolonial Studies* 7.1 (2004): 83–101.

Derrida, Jacques. "Fors: The Anglish Words of Nicholas Abraham and Maria Torok." Introduction. *The Wolf Man's Magic Word: A Cryptonymy*. By Nicolas Abraham and Maria Torok. 1976. Trans. Nicholas Rand. Minneapolis: U of Minnesota P, 1986. xi–xlviii.

———. "Freud's Legacy." *The Post Card: From Socrates to Freud and Beyond*. By Derrida. 1980. Trans. Alan Bass. Chicago: U of Chicago P, 1987. 292–337.

———. "Geopsychoanalysis: '…and the rest of the world.'" Trans. Donald Nicholson-Smith. *The Psychoanalysis of Race*. Ed. Christopher Lane. New York: Columbia UP, 1998. 65–90.

———. "Ja, or the *faux-bond* II." Trans. Peggy Kamuf. *Points…Interviews, 1974–1995*. By Derrida. Ed. Elisabeth Weber. 1992. Stanford: Stanford UP, 1995. 30–77.

———. *Specters of Marx: The State of the Debt, the Work of Mourning, and the New International*. Trans. Peggy Kamuf. New York: Routledge, 1994.

Desai, Anita. *Baumgartner's Bombay*. 1988. London: Vintage, 1998.
———. "A Coat in Many Colours." *South Asian English: Structure, Use and Users*. Ed. Robert J. Baumgardner. Urbana: U of Illinois P, 1996. 221–30.
Döring, Tobias. "Turning the Colonial Gaze: Re-Visions of Terror in Dabydeen's *Turner*." *No Land, No Mother: Essays on the Work of David Dabydeen*. Ed. Kampta Karran and Lynne Macedo. Leeds: Peepal Tree, 2007. 32–47.
Douglas, Kate, and Gillian Whitlock. "Reading Trauma in the Twenty-First Century." Introduction. *Trauma Texts*. Ed. Gillian Whitlock and Kate Douglas. London: Routledge, 2009. 1–8.
Du Bois, W. E. B. "The Negro and the Warsaw Ghetto." *Jewish Life* 6.7 (May 1952): 14–15.
———. *The Souls of Black Folk*. 1903. New York: Vintage, 1990.
———. *The World and Africa: An Inquiry into the Part Which Africa Has Played in World History*. New York: Viking, 1947.
Duran, Eduardo, Bonnie Duran, Maria Yellow Horse Brave Heart, and Susan Yellow Horse-Davis. "Healing the American Indian Soul Wound." *International Handbook of Multigenerational Legacies of Trauma*. Ed. Yael Danieli. New York: Plenum, 1998. 341–54.
Durrant, Sam. *Postcolonial Narrative and the Work of Mourning: J. M. Coetzee, Wilson Harris, and Toni Morrison*. Albany: State U of New York P, 2004.
Eaglestone, Robert. "'You would not add to my suffering if you knew what I have seen': Holocaust Testimony and Contemporary African Trauma Literature." *Postcolonial Trauma Novels*. Ed. Stef Craps and Gert Buelens. Spec. issue of *Studies in the Novel* 40.1–2 (2008): 72–85.
Eagleton, Terry. *Literary Theory: An Introduction*. 2nd ed. Oxford: Blackwell, 1996.
Edkins, Jenny. *Trauma and the Memory of Politics*. Cambridge: Cambridge UP, 2003.
Eggers, Dave. *What Is the What: The Autobiography of Valentino Achak Deng*. San Francisco: McSweeney's, 2006.
Eng, David L., and David Kazanjian. "Mourning Remains." Introduction. *Loss: The Politics of Mourning*. Ed. David L. Eng and David Kazanjian. Berkeley: U of California P, 2003. 1–25.
———, eds. *Loss: The Politics of Mourning*. Berkeley: U of California P, 2003.
Erll, Astrid. "Travelling Memory." *Transcultural Memory*. Ed. Richard Crownshaw. Spec. issue of *Parallax* 17.4 (2011): 4–18.
Falk, Erik. "How to Forget: David Dabydeen's 'Creative Amnesia.'" *Readings of the Particular: The Postcolonial in the Postnational*. Ed. Anne Holden Rønning and Lene Johannessen. Amsterdam: Rodopi, 2007. 187–203.
Fanon, Frantz. *Black Skin, White Masks*. 1952. Trans. Charles Lam Markmann. New York: Grove, 1967.
———. *The Wretched of the Earth*. 1961. Trans. Constance Farrington. New York: Grove, 1963.

Fassin, Didier, and Richard Rechtman. *The Empire of Trauma: An Inquiry into the Condition of Victimhood.* 2007. Trans. Rachel Gomme. Princeton: Princeton UP, 2009.

Feldman, Allen. "Memory Theaters, Virtual Witnessing and the Trauma-Aesthetic." *Biography* 27.1 (2004). *Project MUSE.* 23 Jan. 2008. http://muse.jhu.edu/journals/biography/v027/27.1feldman.html.

Felman, Shoshana, and Dori Laub. *Testimony: Crises of Witnessing in Literature, Psychoanalysis, and History.* New York: Routledge, 1992.

Felski, Rita. *Beyond Feminist Aesthetics: Feminist Literature and Social Change.* Cambridge: Harvard UP, 1989.

Flanzbaum, Hilene, ed. *The Americanization of the Holocaust.* Baltimore: Johns Hopkins UP, 1999.

Flynn, Nick. "Re: 'I Know I'm Not Part of This, but It Kind of Makes You Feel Like You Are.' " Online comment. TPMCafe Book Club. *Talking Points Memo.* 25 Jun. 2008. 31 Dec. 2011. http://tpmcafe.talkingpointsmemo.com/2008/06/25/i_know_im_not_part_of_this_but/index.php#comment-2930317.

Forster, E. M. *A Passage to India.* London: Edward Arnold, 1924.

Frank, Anne. *The Diary of a Young Girl.* 1947. Trans. Susan Massotty. Intro. Elie Wiesel. London: Penguin, 2000.

Freud, Sigmund. "Mourning and Melancholia." *The Standard Edition of the Complete Psychological Works of Sigmund Freud.* Vol. 14. Ed. and trans. James Strachey. London: Hogarth, 1953–74. 243–58.

———. "Screen Memories." *The Standard Edition of the Complete Psychological Works of Sigmund Freud.* Vol. 3. Ed. and trans. James Strachey. London: Hogarth, 1953–74. 303–22.

———. "The Uncanny." *The Standard Edition of the Complete Psychological Works of Sigmund Freud.* Vol. 17. Ed. and trans. James Strachey. London: Hogarth, 1953–74. 218–52.

Frias, Maria. "Building Bridges Back to the Past: An Interview with Fred D'Aguiar." *Callaloo* 25.2 (2002): 418–25.

Friedberg, Lilian. "Dare to Compare: Americanizing the Holocaust." *American Indian Quarterly* 24.3 (2000): 353–80.

Friedrich, Jörg. *The Fire: The Bombing of Germany, 1940–1945.* 2002. Trans. Allison Brown. New York: Columbia UP, 2006.

Furst, Lilian R. *Random Destinations: Escaping the Holocaust and Starting Life Anew.* New York: Palgrave Macmillan, 2005.

Gilroy, Paul. *Between Camps: Nations, Cultures and the Allure of Race.* 2000. London: Routledge, 2004.

———. *The Black Atlantic: Modernity and Double Consciousness.* London: Verso, 1993.

Glissant, Edouard. *Caribbean Discourse: Selected Essays.* Trans. J. Michael Dash. Charlottesville: UP of Virginia, 1989.

———. *Poetics of Relation.* 1990. Trans. Betsy Wing. Ann Arbor: U of Michigan P, 1997.

Gourevitch, Philip. "I Know I'm Not Part of This, but It Kind of Makes You Feel Like You Are." Online post. TPMCafe Book Club. *Talking Points Memo.*

25 June 2008. 31 Dec. 2011. http://tpmcafe.talkingpointsmemo.com/2008/06/25/i_know_im_not_part_of_this_but/.

Gourevitch, Philip, and Errol Morris. *Standard Operating Procedure: A War Story.* London, Picador, 2008.

Graham, Shane. *South African Literature after the Truth Commission: Mapping Loss.* New York: Palgrave Macmillan, 2009.

Gready, Paul. "Novel Truths: Literature and Truth Commissions." *Comparative Literature Studies* 46.1 (2009): 156–76.

Halbwachs, Maurice. *On Collective Memory.* 1950. Ed. and trans. Lewis A. Coser. Chicago: U of Chicago P, 1992.

Hall, Stuart. "When Was 'the Postcolonial'? Thinking at the Limit." *The Post-Colonial Question: Common Skies, Divided Horizons.* Ed. Iain Chambers and Lidia Curti. London: Routledge, 1996. 242–60.

Hamilton, Carrie. "Activist Memories: The Politics of Trauma and the Pleasures of Politics." *The Future of Memory.* Ed. Richard Crownshaw, Jane Kilby, and Antony Rowland. New York: Berghahn, 2010. 265–78.

Hansen, Miriam Bratu. "*Schindler's List* Is Not *Shoah*: The Second Commandment, Popular Modernism, and Public Memory." *Critical Inquiry* 22.2 (1996): 292–312.

Harris, Wilson. *Heartland.* London: Faber and Faber, 1964.

Hartman, Geoffrey H. *The Fateful Question of Culture.* New York: Columbia UP, 1997.

———. "The Humanities of Testimony: An Introduction." *Poetics Today* 27.2 (2006): 249–60.

———. "Memory.com: Tele-Suffering and Testimony in the Dot Com Era." *Raritan* 19.3 (2000): 1–18.

———. "Shoah and Intellectual Witness." *Partisan Review* 65.1 (1998): 37–48.

Henri, Yazir, and Heidi Grunebaum. "Re-historicising Trauma: Reflections on Violence and Memory in Current-day Cape Town." DACPM Occasional Paper Series No. 6. Cape Town: DACPM, 2005.

Herman, Judith Lewis. "Complex PTSD: A Syndrome in Survivors of Prolonged and Repeated Trauma." *Journal of Traumatic Stress* 5.3 (1992): 377–91.

———. *Trauma and Recovery: The Aftermath of Violence—from Domestic Abuse to Political Terror.* New York: Basic, 1992.

Herrero, Dolores, and Sonia Baelo-Allué, eds. *The Splintered Glass: Facets of Trauma in the Post-Colony and Beyond.* Amsterdam: Rodopi, 2011.

Hiddleston, Jane. *Poststructuralism and Postcoloniality: The Anxiety of Theory.* Liverpool: Liverpool UP, 2010.

Hochschild, Adam. *King Leopold's Ghost: A Story of Greed, Terror, and Heroism in Colonial Africa.* New York: Houghton Mifflin, 1998.

Hogan, Patrick Colm. *Empire and Poetic Voice: Cognitive and Cultural Studies of Literary Tradition and Colonialism.* Albany: State U of New York P, 2004.

Huntington, Samuel. "The Clash of Civilizations?" *Foreign Affairs* 72.3 (1993): 22–49.

Hutcheon, Linda. "Rethinking the National Model." *Rethinking Literary History: A Dialogue on Theory.* Ed. Linda Hutcheon and Mario J. Valdés. Oxford: Oxford UP, 2002. 3–49.

Huyssen, Andreas. "The Politics of Identification: 'Holocaust' and West German Drama." *After the Great Divide: Modernism, Mass Culture, Postmodernism.* By Huyssen. Bloomington: Indiana UP, 1986. 94–114.

———. *Present Pasts: Urban Palimpsests and the Politics of Memory.* Stanford: Stanford UP, 2003.

———. "Resistance to Memory: The Uses and Abuses of Public Forgetting." *Globalizing Critical Theory.* Ed. Max Pensky. Lanham: Rowman and Littlefield, 2005. 165–84.

Iraq Body Count. 10 Feb. 2012. http://www.iraqbodycount.org/.

Irizarry, Estelle. "Three Sources of Textual Evidence of Columbus, Crypto Jew." *Tbspr.org.* Apr. 2006. 1 Mar. 2012. http://www.tbspr.org/_kd/Items/actions. cfm?action= Show&item_id= 2026.

Iweala, Uzodinma. *Beasts of No Nation.* London: John Murray, 2005.

Jameson, Fredric. *The Political Unconscious: Narrative as a Socially Symbolic Act.* Ithaca: Cornell UP, 1981.

Janoff-Bulman, Ronnie. *Shattered Assumptions: Towards a New Psychology of Trauma.* New York: Free, 1992.

Jay, Martin. "Allegories of Evil: A Response to Jeffrey Alexander." *Remembering the Holocaust: A Debate.* By Jeffrey C. Alexander et al. Oxford: Oxford UP, 2009. 105–13.

Jussawalla, Feroza F. "Anita Desai." *Interviews with Writers of the Post-Colonial World.* Ed. Feroza F. Jussawalla and Reed Way Dasenbrock. Jackson: UP of Mississippi, 1992. 156–79.

K, Dan. "Re: 'I Know I'm Not Part of This, but It Kind of Makes You Feel Like You Are.'" Online comment. TPMCafe Book Club. *Talking Points Memo.* 25 Jun. 2008. 31 Dec. 2011. http://tpmcafe.talkingpointsmemo.com/2008/06/25/i_know_im_not_part_of_this_but/index.php#comment-2928411.

Kacandes, Irene. "Testimony: Talk as Witnessing." *Talk Fiction: Literature and the Talk Explosion.* By Kacandes. Lincoln: U of Nebraska P, 2001. 89–140.

Kalmar, Ivan Davidson, and Derek J. Penslar. "Orientalism and the Jews: An Introduction." *Orientalism and the Jews.* Ed. Kalmar and Penslar. Lebanon: Brandeis UP, 2005. xiii–xl.

Kaplan, E. Ann. "Fanon, Trauma and Cinema." *Frantz Fanon: Critical Perspectives.* Ed. Anthony C. Alessandrini. London: Routledge, 1999. 146–58,

———. *Trauma Culture: The Politics of Terror and Loss in Media and Literature.* New Brunswick: Rutgers UP, 2005.

Kennedy, Rosanne. "Mortgaged Futures: Trauma, Subjectivity, and the Legacies of Colonialism in Tsitsi Dangarembga's *The Book of Not.*" *Postcolonial Trauma Novels.* Ed. Stef Craps and Gert Buelens. Spec. issue of *Studies in the Novel* 40.1–2 (2008): 86–107.

Kennedy, Rosanne, and Tikka Jan Wilson. "Constructing Shared Histories: Stolen Generations Testimony, Narrative Therapy and Address." *World*

Memory: Personal Trajectories in Global Time. Ed. Jill Bennett and Rosanne Kennedy. Houndmills: Palgrave Macmillan, 2003. 119–39.

Khanna, Ranjana. *Dark Continents: Pyschoanalysis and Colonialism.* Durham: Duke UP, 2003.

Kilby, Jane. "The Future of Trauma." Introduction. *The Future of Memory.* Ed. Richard Crownshaw, Jane Kilby, and Antony Rowland. New York: Berghahn, 2010. 181–90.

King, Richard H., and Dan Stone, eds. *Hannah Arendt and the Uses of History: Imperialism, Nation, Race, and Genocide.* New York: Berghahn, 2007.

LaCapra, Dominick. *History and Its Limits: Human, Animal, Violence.* Ithaca: Cornell UP, 2009.

———. *History and Memory after Auschwitz.* Ithaca: Cornell UP, 1998.

———. *History in Transit: Experience, Identity, Critical Theory.* Ithaca: Cornell UP, 2004.

———. *Representing the Holocaust: History, Theory, Trauma.* Ithaca: Cornell UP, 1994.

———. *Writing History, Writing Trauma.* Baltimore: Johns Hopkins UP, 2001.

Lambek, Michael, and Paul Antze. "Forecasting Memory." Introduction. *Tense Past: Cultural Essays in Trauma and Memory.* Ed. Paul Antze and Michael Lambek. London: Routledge, 1996. xi–xxxviii.

Landsberg, Alison. *Prosthetic Memory: The Transformation of American Remembrance in the Age of Mass Culture.* New York: Columbia UP, 2004.

Lane, Christopher. "The Pyschoanalysis of Race: An Introduction." *The Psychoanalysis of Race.* Ed. Lane. New York: Columbia UP, 1998. 1–37.

Lazarus, Neil. *Nationalism and Cultural Practice in the Postcolonial World.* Cambridge: Cambridge UP, 1999.

Ledent, Bénédicte. *Caryl Phillips.* Manchester: Manchester UP, 2002.

Lerner, Paul, and Mark S. Micale. "Trauma, Psychiatry, and History: A Conceptual and Historiographical Introduction." *Traumatic Pasts: History, Psychiatry, and Trauma in the Modern Age, 1870–1930.* Ed. Mark S. Micale and Paul Lerner. Cambridge: Cambridge UP, 2001. 1–27.

Levi, Neil. "'No Sensible Comparison'? The Place of the Holocaust in Australia's History Wars." *History and Memory* 19.1 (2007): 124–56.

Levi, Primo. *If This Is a Man.* 1947. Trans. Stuart Woolf. New York: Orion, 1959.

Levy, Daniel, and Natan Sznaider. *The Holocaust and Memory in the Global Age.* 2001. Trans. Assenka Oksiloff. Philadelphia: Temple UP, 2006.

Leys, Ruth. *Trauma: A Genealogy.* Chicago: U of Chicago P, 2000.

Linenthal, Edward T. *Preserving Memory: The Struggle to Create America's Holocaust Museum.* New York: Viking, 1995.

Long Night's Journey into Day. Dir. Frances Reid and Deborah Hoffmann. DVD. Iris Films, 2000.

López, Alfred J. "The Gaze of the White Wolf: Psychoanalysis, Whiteness, and Colonial Trauma." *Postcolonial Whiteness: A Critical Reader on Race and Empire.* Ed. López. Albany: State U of New York P, 2005. 155–81.

Luckhurst, Roger. *The Trauma Question.* London: Routledge, 2008.

Lund, Giuliana "'Healing the Nation': Medicolonial Discourse and the State of Emergency from Apartheid to Truth and Reconciliation." *Cultural Critique* 54 (2003): 88–119.

Magona, Sindiwe. *Mother to Mother.* 1998. Boston: Beacon, 1999.

———. "Two Little Girls and a City." *Living, Loving, and Lying Awake at Night.* By Magona. 1991. Northampton: Interlink, 2009. 117–42.

Maier, Charles S. "Consigning the Twentieth Century to History: Alternative Narratives for the Modern Era." *American Historical Review* 105.3 (2000): 807–31.

Mamdani, Mahmood. "Amnesty or Impunity? A Preliminary Critique of the Report of the Truth and Reconciliation Commission of South Africa (TRC)." *Diacritics* 32.3–4 (2002): 33–59.

———. "Reconciliation without Justice." *Southern African Review of Books* 46 (Dec. 1996): 3–5.

Manne, Robert. "On the Political Corruptions of a Moral Universal." *Remembering the Holocaust: A Debate.* By Jeffrey C. Alexander et al. Oxford: Oxford UP, 2009. 135–45.

Mantel, Hilary. "Black Is Not Jewish." Rev. of *The Nature of Blood*, by Caryl Phillips. *Literary Review* 1 Feb. 1997: 39.

Margalit, Avishai. *The Ethics of Memory.* Cambridge: Harvard UP, 2002.

Matus, Jill. *Toni Morrison.* Manchester: Manchester UP, 1998.

Mazower, Mark. *Hitler's Empire: Nazi Rule in Occupied Europe.* London: Allen Lane, 2008.

McClintock, Anne. "The Angel of Progress: Pitfalls of the Term 'Post-Colonialism.'" *Social Text* 10.2–3 (1992): 84–98.

McNally, Richard J. "Conceptual Problems with the DSM-IV Criteria for Posttraumatic Stress Disorder." *Posttraumatic Stress Disorder: Issues and Controversies.* Ed. Gerald M. Rosen. Chichester: Wiley, 2004. 1–14.

Micale, Mark S., and Paul Lerner, eds. *Traumatic Pasts: History, Psychiatry, and Trauma in the Modern Age, 1870–1930.* Cambridge: Cambridge UP, 2001.

Moglen, Seth. "On Mourning Social Injury." *Psychoanalysis, Culture and Society* 10 (2005): 151–67.

Moi, Toril. *Sexual/Textual Politics: Feminist Literary Theory.* London: Routledge, 1985.

Morrison, Toni. *Beloved.* New York: Knopf, 1987.

Morton, Stephen. "Poststructuralist Formulations." *The Routledge Companion to Postcolonial Studies.* Ed. John McLeod. London: Routledge, 2007. 161–72.

Moses, A. Dirk. "Conceptual Blockages and Definitional Dilemmas in the 'Racial Century': Genocides of Indigenous Peoples and the Holocaust." *Patterns of Prejudice* 36.4 (2002): 7–36.

———. "Genocide and the Terror of History." *Transcultural Memory.* Ed. Richard Crownshaw. Spec. issue of *Parallax* 17.4 (2011): 90–108.

Moshman, David. "Conceptual Constraints on Thinking about Genocide." *Journal of Genocide Research* 3.3 (2001): 431–50.

Mufti, Aamir R. *Enlightenment in the Colony: The Jewish Question and the Crisis of Postcolonial Culture.* Princeton: Princeton UP, 2007.

Nasser, Latif. "Do Some Cultures Have Their Own Ways of Going Mad?" *Boston Globe* 8 Jan. 2012. 15 Jan. 2012. http://articles.boston.com/2012-01-08/ideas/30596717_1_mental-illness-cultural-sensitivity-appendix.

Nora, Pierre. *Realms of Memory: Rethinking the French Past.* 1984–1992. Ed. Lawrence D. Kritzman. Trans. Arthur Goldhammer. 3 vols. New York: Columbia UP, 1996–1998.

Novak, Amy. "Who Speaks? Who Listens? The Problem of Address in Two Nigerian Trauma Novels." *Postcolonial Trauma Novels.* Ed. Stef Craps and Gert Buelens. Spec. issue of *Studies in the Novel* 40.1–2 (2008): 31–51.

Novick, Peter. *The Holocaust in American Life.* New York: Houghton Mifflin, 1999.

Nowak, Helge. "'Naturally, Their Suffering Is Deeply Connected to Memory': Caryl Phillips's *The Nature of Blood* as a Grand Narrative of Racism and Xenophobia." *Xenophobic Memories: Otherness in Postcolonial Constructions of the Past.* Ed. Monika Gomille and Klaus Stierstorfer. Heidelberg: Universitätsverlag Winter, 2003. 115–33.

Orantes, Karin. "The Magic of Writing: An Interview with Sindiwe Magona." *Trauma, Memory, and Narrative in South Africa: Interviews.* Ed. Ewald Mengel, Michela Borzaga, and Karin Orantes. Amsterdam: Rodopi, 2010. 31–48.

Ozick, Cynthia. *The Shawl.* New York: Random House, 1990.

Pandit, Lalita. "A Sense of Detail and a Sense of Order: Anita Desai Interviewed by Lalita Pandit." *Literary India: Comparative Studies in Aesthetics, Colonialism, and Culture.* Ed. Patrick Colm Hogan and Lalita Pandit. Albany: State U of New York P, 1995. 153–72.

Parry, Benita. *Postcolonial Studies: A Materialist Critique.* London: Routledge, 2004.

Philip, M. NourbeSe. *Zong!* Toronto: Mercury, 2008.

Phillips, Caryl. "Anne Frank's Amsterdam." *The European Tribe.* By Phillips. London: Faber and Faber, 1987. 66–71.

———. *The Atlantic Sound.* London: Faber and Faber, 2000.

———. "A Black European Success." *The European Tribe.* By Phillips. London: Faber and Faber, 1987. 45–51.

———. *Crossing the River.* London: Bloomsbury, 1993.

———. *A Distant Shore.* London: Secker and Warburg, 2003.

———. "The Gift of Displacement". Introduction. *A New World Order: Selected Essays.* By Phillips. London: Secker and Warburg, 2001. 129–34.

———. *Higher Ground: A Novel in Three Parts.* New York: Viking Penguin, 1989.

———. "In the Ghetto". *The European Tribe.* By Phillips. London: Faber and Faber, 1987. 52–55.

———. *The Nature of Blood.* London: Faber and Faber, 1997.

———. "On 'The Nature of Blood' and the Ghost of Anne Frank." *CommonQuest* 3.2 (1998): 4–7.

Poole, Ross. "Misremembering the Holocaust: Universal Symbol, Nationalist Icon or Moral Kitsch?" *Memory and the Future: Transnational Politics,*

Ethics and Society. Ed. Yifat Gutman, Adam D. Brown, and Amy Sodaro. Houndmills: Palgrave Macmillan, 2010. 31–49.

Poussaint, Alvin F., and Amy Alexander. *Lay My Burden Down: Suicide and the Mental Health Crisis Among African-Americans*. Boston: Beacon, 2000.

Radstone, Susannah. "Trauma Theory: Contexts, Politics, Ethics." *Paragraph: A Journal of Modern Critical Theory* 30.1 (2007): 9–29.

Ricciardi, Alessia. *The Ends of Mourning: Pyschoanalysis, Literature, Film*. Stanford: Stanford UP, 2003.

Rodriguez, Phyllis, and Aicha el-Wafi. "9/11 Healing: The Mothers Who Found Forgiveness, Friendship." *TEDWomen*. Filmed Dec. 2010. Posted May 2011. *TED Talks*. 30 Dec. 2011. http://www.ted.com/talks/9_11_healing_the_mothers_who_found_forgiveness_friendship.html.

Root, Maria P. P. "Reconstructing the Impact of Trauma on Personality." *Personality and Psychopathology: Feminist Reappraisals*. Ed. Laura S. Brown and Mary Ballou. New York: Guilford, 1992. 229–65.

Rosen, Gerald M., Robert L. Spitzer, and Paul R. McHugh. "Problems with the Post-Traumatic Stress Disorder Diagnosis and Its Future in DSM–V." *British Journal of Psychiatry* 192.1 (2008): 3–4. doi: 10.1192/bjp.bp.107.043083.

Rosenfeld, Alvin H. "The Americanization of the Holocaust." *Commentary* 99.6 (1995): 35–40.

Rothberg, Michael. "From Gaza to Warsaw: Mapping Multidirectional Memory." *Transcultural Negotiations of Holocaust Memory*. Ed. Stef Craps and Michael Rothberg. Spec. issue of *Criticism: A Quarterly for Literature and the Arts* 53.4 (2011): 523–48.

———. "Multidirectional Memory and the Universalization of the Holocaust." *Remembering the Holocaust: A Debate*. By Jeffrey C. Alexander et al. Oxford: Oxford UP, 2009. 123–34.

———. *Multidirectional Memory: Remembering the Holocaust in the Age of Decolonization*. Stanford: Stanford UP, 2009.

———. *Traumatic Realism: The Demands of Holocaust Representation*. Minneapolis: U of Minnesota P, 2000.

Rothberg, Michael, Debarati Sanyal, and Max Silverman, eds. *Nœuds de Mémoire: Multidirectional Memory in Postwar French and Francophone Culture*. Spec. issue of *Yale French Studies* 118–19 (2010).

Said, Edward W. *Freud and the Non-European*. London: Verso, 2003.

Samuelson, Meg. "The Mother as Witness: Reading *Mother to Mother* alongside South Africa's Truth and Reconciliation Commission." *Sindiwe Magona: The First Decade*. Ed. Siphokazi Koyana. Scottsville: U of KwaZulu-Natal P, 2004. 127–44.

———. "Reading the Maternal Voice in Sindiwe Magona's *To My Children's Children* and *Mother to Mother*." *Modern Fiction Studies* 46.1 (2000): 227–45.

———. *Remembering the Nation, Dismembering Women? Stories of the South African Transition*. Scottsville: U of Kwazulu-Natal P, 2007.

Saunders, Rebecca. *Lamentation and Modernity in Literature, Philosophy, and Culture*. New York: Palgrave Macmillan, 2007.

Saunders, Rebecca, and Kamran Aghaie. "Mourning and Memory." Introduction. *Mourning and Memory*. Ed. Saunders and Aghaie. Spec. section of

Comparative Studies of South Asia, Africa and the Middle East 25.1 (2005): 16–29.

——, eds. *Mourning and Memory*. Spec. section of *Comparative Studies of South Asia, Africa and the Middle East* 25.1 (2005).

Schaffer, Kay. "Memory, Narrative and Forgiveness: Reflecting on Ten Years of South Africa's Truth and Reconciliation Commission, University of Cape Town, 23–27 November 2006." *Borderlands E-Journal* 5.3 (2006): n. pag. 23 Jan. 2008. http://www.borderlandsejournal.adelaide.edu.au/vol5no3_2006/schaffer_memory.htm.

——. "Response to Jaco Barnard." *Borderlands E-Journal* 6.1 (2007): n. pag. 23 Jan. 2008. http://www.borderlandsejournal.adelaide.edu.au/vol6no1_2007/schaffer_response.htm.

Schwarz-Bart, André. *The Last of the Just*. 1959. Trans. Stephen Becker. New York: Atheneum, 1961.

Seltzer, Mark. "Wound Culture: Trauma in the Pathological Public Sphere." *October* 80 (Spring 1997): 3–26.

Semelin, Jacques. *Purify and Destroy: The Political Uses of Massacre and Genocide*. Trans. Cynthia Schoch. New York: Columbia UP, 2007.

Shohat, Ella. "Notes on the 'Post-Colonial.'" *Social Text* 10.2–3 (1992): 99–113.

Sicher, Efraim, and Linda Weinhouse. "The Jew's Passage to India: Desai, Rushdie and Globalised Culture." *European Review of History: Revue européenne d'histoire* 18.1 (2011): 21–31.

Silverman, Max. "Interconnected Histories: Holocaust and Empire in the Cultural Imaginary." *French Studies* 62.4 (2008): 417–28.

Snyder, Timothy. *Bloodlands: Europe between Hitler and Stalin*. New York: Basic, 2010.

Spanierman, Lisa B., and V. Paul Poteat. "Moving Beyond Complacency to Commitment: Multicultural Research in Counseling Psychology." *Counseling Psychologist* 33 (2005): 513–23.

Stocks, Claire. "Trauma Theory and the Singular Self: Rethinking Extreme Experiences in the Light of Cross Cultural Identity." *Textual Practice* 21.1 (2007): 71–92.

Stone, Dan. "The Historiography of Genocide: Beyond 'Uniqueness' and Ethnic Competition." *Rethinking History* 8.1 (2004): 127–42.

Straker, Gill, and the Sanctuaries Counselling Team. "The Continuous Traumatic Stress Syndrome: The Single Therapeutic Interview." *Psychology in Society* 8 (1987): 48–79.

Summerfield, Derek. "A Critique of Seven Assumptions behind Psychological Trauma Programmes in War-Affected Areas." *Social Science and Medicine* 48 (1999): 1449–62.

——. "Cross-Cultural Perspectives on the Medicalization of Human Suffering." *Posttraumatic Stress Disorder: Issues and Controversies*. Ed. Gerald M. Rosen. Chichester: Wiley, 2004. 233–45.

Syrotinski, Michael. *Deconstruction and the Postcolonial: At the Limits of Theory*. Liverpool: Liverpool UP, 2007.

Tal, Kalí. "Remembering Difference: Working against Eurocentric Bias in Contemporary Scholarship on Trauma and Memory." *Worlds of Hurt: Reading the Literatures of Trauma*. Cambridge: Cambridge UP, 1996. Online-only chapter published in 2003. 11 Mar. 2010. http://www.freshmonsters.com/kalital/Text/Worlds/Chap3.html.

———. *Worlds of Hurt: Reading the Literatures of Trauma*. Cambridge: Cambridge UP, 1996.

Terr, Lenore C. "Childhood Traumas: An Outline and Overview." *American Journal of Psychiatry* 148 (1991): 10–20.

Thomas, Helen. *Caryl Phillips*. Tavistock: Northcote/British Council, 2006.

Traverso, Antonio, and Mick Broderick, eds. *Interrogating Trauma: Arts and Media Responses to Collective Suffering*. Spec. issue of *Continuum: Journal of Media and Cultural Studies* 24.1 (2010). Repr. as Traverso, Antonio, and Mick Broderick, eds. *Interrogating Trauma: Collective Suffering in Global Arts and Media*. London: Routledge, 2010.

Truth and Reconciliation Commission of South Africa. *Truth and Reconciliation Commission of South Africa Interim Report*. Cape Town: Truth and Reconciliation Commission, 1996.

———. *Truth and Reconciliation Commission of South Africa Report*. Cape Town: Truth and Reconciliation Commission, 1998. 30 Dec. 2011. http://www.doj.gov.za/trc/report/.

Turia, Tariana. "Tariana Turia's Speech Notes." Speech to NZ Psychological Society Conference 2000, Waikato University, Hamilton, 29 Aug. 2000. 11 Mar. 2010. http://www.converge.org.nz/pma/tspeech.htm.

van der Kolk, Bessel, and Onno van der Hart. "The Intrusive Past: The Flexibility of Memory and the Engraving of Trauma." *Trauma: Explorations in Memory*. Ed. Cathy Caruth. Baltimore: Johns Hopkins UP, 1995. 158–82.

Vergès, Françoise. "Chains of Madness, Chains of Colonialism: Fanon and Freedom." *The Fact of Blackness: Frantz Fanon and Visual Representation*. Ed. Alan Read. London: Institute of Contemporary Arts, 1996. 46–75.

Vermeulen, Pieter. "Video Testimony, Modernity, and the Claims of Melancholia." *Transcultural Negotiations of Holocaust Memory*. Ed. Stef Craps and Michael Rothberg. Spec. issue of *Criticism: A Quarterly for Literature and the Arts* 53.4 (2011): 549–68.

Walkowitz, Rebecca K. "Comparison Literature." *New Literary History* 40.3 (2009): 567–82.

———. "The Location of Literature." *Contemporary Literature* 47.4 (2006): 527–45.

Ward, Abigail. *Caryl Phillips, David Dabydeen and Fred D'Aguiar: Representations of Slavery*. Manchester: Manchester UP, 2011.

Warner, Marina. *Indigo*. New York: Simon and Schuster, 1992.

Watters, Ethan. "The Americanization of Mental Illness." *New York Times Magazine* 8 Jan. 2010. 11 Mar. 2010. http://www.nytimes.com/2010/01/10/magazine/10psyche-t.html.

———. *Crazy Like Us: The Globalization of the American Psyche*. New York: Free, 2010.

Wessells, Michael G. "Culture, Power, and Community: Intercultural Approaches to Psychosocial Assistance and Healing." *Honoring Differences: Cultural Issues in the Treatment of Trauma and Loss*. Ed. Kathleen Nader, Nancy Dubrow, and Beth Hudnall Stamm. Philadelphia: Brunner/Mazel, 1999. 267–82.

White, Hayden. *Metahistory: The Historical Imagination in Nineteenth-Century Europe*. Baltimore: Johns Hopkins UP, 1973.

Whitehead, Anne. *Trauma Fiction*. Edinburgh: Edinburgh UP, 2004.

Whitlock, Gillian, and Kate Douglas, eds. *Trauma Texts*. London: Routledge, 2009.

Wiesel, Elie. *Un di velt hot geshvign (And the World Remained Silent)*. Buenos Aires: Tsentral-Farband fun Poylische Yidn in Argentine, 1956.

Wiesenthal, Simon. *Sails of Hope: The Secret Mission of Christopher Columbus*. 1972. Trans. Richard Winston and Clara Winston. New York: Macmillan, 1973.

Wilder, Gary. "Race, Reason, Impasse: Césaire, Fanon, and the Legacy of Emancipation." *Radical History Review* 90 (Fall 2004): 31–61.

Wilson, John P. "The Historical Evolution of PTSD Diagnostic Criteria: From Freud to DSM-IV." *Journal of Traumatic Stress* 7.4 (1994): 681–98.

Winter, Jay. "The Generation of Memory: Reflections on the 'Memory Boom' in Contemporary Historical Studies." *Bulletin of the German Historical Institute* 27 (Fall 2000): 69–92.

Wood, Nancy. *Vectors of Memory: Legacies of Trauma in Postwar Europe*. Oxford: Berg, 1999.

Yelin, Louise. "'Our Broken Word': Fred D'Aguiar, David Dabydeen, and the Slave Ship Zong." *Revisiting Slave Narratives/Les avatars contemporains des récits d'esclaves*. Ed. Judith Misrahi-Barak. Les Carnets du Cerpac 2. Montpellier: Université Montpellier III, 2005. 349–63.

Young, Allan. *The Harmony of Illusions: Inventing Post-Traumatic Stress Disorder*. Princeton: Princeton UP, 1995.

Young, Robert J. C. "Deconstruction and the Postcolonial." *Deconstructions: A User's Guide*. Ed. Nicholas Royle. London: Palgrave, 2000. 187–210.

———. *Postcolonialism: An Historical Introduction*. Malden: Blackwell, 2001.

———. *White Mythologies: Writing History and the West*. London: Routledge, 1990.

Zierler, Wendy. "'My Holocaust Is Not Your Holocaust': 'Facing' Black and Jewish Experience in *The Pawnbroker, Higher Ground*, and *The Nature of Blood*." *Holocaust and Genocide Studies* 18.1 (2004): 46–67.

Zimmerer, Jurgen. "The Birth of the *Ostland* out of the Spirit of Colonialism: A Postcolonial Perspective on the Nazi Policy of Conquest and Extermination." *Patterns of Prejudice* 39.2 (2005): 197–219.

Index

Abani, Christopher, 42
ableism, 25–26
abolition, of slavery, 64, 67
Aborigines, 42
abortion, 66, 75
abortion Holocaust, 75
Abraham, Nicolas, 62
absence, and loss, distinction
    between, 4, 31–32, 133
Abu Ghraib scandal, 128–30
abuse
    child, 53, 62, 65, 69, 92, 136
    domestic, 21, 27, 52, 115, 125,
        137
    human rights, 44, 47, 75, 77, 78,
        135
    prisoner, 128–30
    racial, 5, 8, 21, 26, 28, 29, 30, 32,
        34, 42, 45, 65, 71, 83, 126
    sexual, 21, 25–26, 27, 61
acceptance, 23, 81, 94, 100, 105,
    110, 112, 117
accident, 16–17, 31
Achebe, Chinua, 119
activism, 21, 24, 26, 49, 126, 127,
    140
Adichie, Chimamanda Ngozi, 42
Adorno, Theodor
    "Commitment," 39–40
    "Cultural Criticism and Society,"
        33
aeroplane crashes, 24
African Holocaust, 10, 75
agency, 28, 36, 47, 96, 129,
    140
aggression, 26, 125, 130
Aghaie, Kamran, 140
Ahmad, Aijaz, 35, 36
Alexander, Amy, 25

Alexander, Jeffrey C.
    "The Dilemma of Uniqueness,"
        83
    Remembering the Holocaust: A
        Debate, 75, 76–77, 137
    Trauma: A Social Theory, 137
Algeria, 29, 36, 84, 86
Algerian War of Independence
    (1954–1962), 36, 86
alienation, 30–31, 91
Allied bombing, 78
Althusser, Louis, 36
American Holocaust, 75
Americanization of the Holocaust,
    74, 83, 86
American Psychiatric Association,
    23, 25
amnesty, 49, 58
Amy Biehl Foundation, 49
Amy Biehl killing, *see* Biehl, Amy
analogy, 16, 18–19, 39, 62, 75, 83,
    91, 95, 97, 100, 111,
    138
anamnestic solidarity, 60
anger, 46, 51–52, 66, 133
    see also outrage
anorexia, 22
anti-colonial liberation, 36, 82
anti-narrative texts, 4–5, 40–41
anti-Semitism, 7, 84, 89, 92,
    138
anxiety disorders, 23
apartheid, 5, 10, 44–49, 52, 54–58,
    60, 124, 133, 135
Arendt, Hannah, 84, 138
arrest, 57, 98, 109
Arruti, Nerea, 9
Assmann, Aleida, 73, 74, 80

Assmann, Jan
  Das kulturelle Gedächtnis: Schrift,
    Erinnerung, und Identität in den
    frühen Hochkulturen, 73
  Moses the Egyptian: The Memory of
    Egypt in Western Monotheism,
    17
atomic bombing of
  Hiroshima/Nagasaki, 10, 18–19,
    130–31
atrocities, 6, 10, 75, 78, 80, 84, 85,
    93, 98, 135, 137
Auschwitz, 39, 40, 75, 90, 99
avant-garde texts, 5, 38, 39–41
aversive bias, 26
  see also bias
Azanian People's Liberation Army,
    58

Baelo-Allué, Sonia, 140
Ball, Karyn, 72
barbarism, 39–40, 55, 118, 119
Barnard, Jaco, 134–35
Bataille, Georges, 130
battered women, 21
Baucom, Ian, 68
Beah, Ishmael, 42
Beckett, Samuel, 40, 134
belatedness, 15, 16, 63
belonging, 84, 87, 97, 106, 113–14
Bennett, Jill, 13, 39, 41, 139
Bergen-Belsen, 90, 98
Bergner, Gwen, 27, 132
Berlant, Lauren, 124, 125, 126, 140
Bettelheim, Bruno, 99
Bhabha, Homi K., 35, 36
bias, 2, 4, 12, 14, 26–27, 32, 33–34,
    35, 44, 80, 124, 132
Biehl, Amy, 5, 49, 52, 54, 55, 58, 135
Biehl, Linda, 49, 50
Biehl, Peter, 49
body, 29–30, 53, 64–65, 122, 124–25,
    139
Boehmer, Elleke, 58–59
Bombay, 102, 103, 104, 108, 112,
    113, 114, 115, 118

bondage, *see* slavery
boomerang thesis, 84, 138
Bracken, Patrick J., 131
Brink, André, 44
British imperialism, 11–12, 110
Broderick, Mick, 140
Brown, Laura S.
  Cultural Competence in Trauma
    Therapy: Beyond the Flashback,
    24, 25, 26–27, 131, 132
  "Not Outside the Range: One
    Feminist Perspective on
    Psychic Trauma," 21, 31, 33
Brown, Wendy, 124, 125–26
Bryant-Davis, Thema, 26, 27
Buddhism, 23, 79
Buelens, Gert, 140
Burrows, Victoria, 32, 63, 130,
    132–33, 139
Bush, George W., 78
Butler, Judith, 13, 127

calamity, 72, 114
Calcutta, 103, 119
  famine, 1943, 111
  pre-Partition violence, 7, 102, 110,
    111, 112
camp-thinking, 7, 106–07, 122, 123
cannibalism, 65, 119, 121, 122
capitalism, 35, 61, 63
car crashes, 125
Caruth, Cathy
  cross-cultural encounters, 3,
    14–19, 72, 130
  epistemological/ethical
    programme of trauma theory,
    1–2
  focus on Holocaust, 3, 9
  incomparability of traumas, 100
  modernist aesthetic, 40
  perpetrator trauma, 130
  punctual trauma model, 31
  Trauma: Explorations in Memory,
    10, 31, 101, 130

Luckhurst, Roger, 39, 41, 132
Lund, Giuliana, 148
Lyndi Fourie Foundation, 58
Lyotard, Jean-François, 36

Magona, Sindiwe
  Mother to Mother, 5, 44, 48–59, 60,
    72, 135
  "Two Little Girls and a City,"
    50–51, 52
Maier, Charles S., 137
Mamdani, Mahmood, 45
Manne, Robert, 77–78, 137
Manqina, Evelyn, 49
Manqina, Mongezi Christopher, 49,
    50
Mantel, Hilary, 139
Margalit, Avishai, 80
marginalization, 2, 3, 30, 75, 80,
    114, 115
Marx, Karl, 62
Marxism, 35, 116, 117, 134
masochism, 125
massacre
  Heidelberg Tavern massacre, 1993,
    58
  Sharpville massacre, 1960, 135
  Zong massacre, 1781, 64, 67–71,
    135–36
materialism, 13, 30–31, 35, 46, 48,
    56, 57, 132
Mazower, Mark, 84
McClintock, Anne, 63
McNally, Richard J., 25
media, 26, 40, 43, 46–47, 49, 51, 70,
    74, 140
melancholia, 60, 62, 66, 133
memoirs, 41, 42, 100
memory
  boom, 73
  collective, 18–19, 43, 65, 67,
    73–74, 77, 85, 86–87
  cosmopolitan, 74, 117
  cultural, 73
  globalization of, 73–88, 127, 137

multidirectional, 85–88, 91, 111,
    121
  personal, 19
  politics of, 61, 63, 83, 87–88
  prosthetic, 74
  public, 43, 86, 87
  screen, 79, 83, 137
  see also Holocaust
metaphor, 7, 30, 32, 36, 47, 63, 76,
    77–78, 89, 90, 91, 95, 97, 100,
    106, 118–19, 138
metonymy, 7, 89, 91, 97, 100–01,
    108
Micale, Mark S., 20
microaggressions, 26
  see also racism
Middle Passage
  in Dabydeen's "Turner," 5, 60,
    64–66
  in D'Aguiar's *Feeding the Ghosts,* 5,
    60, 67–71, 137
  as founding trauma, 136
  in Morrison's *Beloved,* 136
mid-mourning, 62–63, 133, 136
migration, 7, 74, 92, 97, 102, 103,
    111, 114
militancy, 49, 94, 127
Milosevic, Slobodan, 75
mirroring, 21, 55, 95, 106, 115
misogyny, 133
modernism, 2, 4–5, 6, 7, 11, 12,
    39–41, 43
modernity, 2, 7, 12, 35, 81, 84, 89,
    96, 106, 110, 118
modernization, resistance to,
    128
Moglen, Seth, 133
Moi, Toril, 38
monocultural bias, 24, 44
  see also bias
monotheism, 16
morality, 15, 20, 26, 40, 67, 74–75,
    77, 78, 80, 86, 87–88, 117, 129,
    137
Morris, Errol, 128–30
Morrison, Toni, 71, 136

70994986R00104

Made in the USA
Middletown, DE
19 April 2018